LIGHT FOR THE SEEKER

For sidi Muhammad Iqbal Khan.

بارك الله فيكم وزادكم نوراً وهدى.

– Samer

Published in the UK by
Beacon Books and Media Ltd
Innospace, The Shed
Chester Street
Manchester
M1 5GD

www.beaconbooks.net

Typesetting & Cover art by Etherea Design

Printed in the UK

ISBN 978-0-9954960-6-4

A CIP catalogue record for this book is available from the British Library.

Light for the Seeker

A DAILY LITANY OF FORTY
SALAWAT & OTHER SUPPLICATIONS

SHAYKH SALIH AL-JAᶜFARI &
SHAYKH ᶜABD AL-GHANI AL-JAᶜFARI

BEACON BOOKS

Contents

Introduction
1

Commencement of the Gathering
7

Forty Ṣalawāt
11

Thirty Ṣalawāt for Easing that which has been Decreed
67

The Opener of Locks
75

The Prayer for Swift Relief and Ease
83

Ninety-Nine Names of Allāh
97

The Qur'ānic Defences
105

The Supplications of Praise
111

The Prayer of Wondrous Relief & Quick Opening
115

Introduction

On one night, when two thirds of the night had passed and the last third remained, the Messenger of Allāh, our master Muhammad ﷺ got up to wake up those of his Companions who were sleeping. He urged them to prepare themselves for death and the Day of Resurrection by engaging in the Remembrance of Allāh at that part of the night. Upon hearing this, Ubayy ibn Kaʿb ﷺ approached the Messenger of Allāh and said to him, 'O Messenger of Allāh, I engage in a lot of supplication at night, and I usually spend much of it asking Allāh to exalt you, so how much of my supplications should be dedicated to that?'

The Messenger of Allāh ﷺ said, 'Whatever you wish.'

Ubayy said, 'A quarter of my supplications?'

The Messenger of Allāh ﷺ said, 'As you wish. If you do more, that would be better for you.'

Ubayy said, 'Half?'

The Messenger of Allāh ﷺ said, 'As you wish. If you do more, that would be better for you.'

Ubayy said, 'Two thirds?'

The Messenger of Allāh ﷺ said, 'As you wish. If you do more, that would be better for you.'

Ubayy said, 'Then I will dedicate all my time to asking Allāh to exalt you.'

The Messenger of Allāh ﷺ said, 'If you do that, everything that worries you will be taken care of, and all your sins will be forgiven.' According to another narration the Messenger of Allāh ﷺ said, 'Allāh will take care of all that worries you, whether it be from the affairs of this world or the next.'[1]

The invocation of Allāh's *ṣalawāt* upon our master Muḥammad ﷺ is one of the greatest and most rewarding of acts. He ﷺ said, 'Whoever asks Allāh to exalt me once, Allāh will exalt him ten times for it.'[2] The Knower of Allāh, Shaykh ʿAbd al-Ghanī al-Jaʿfarī ؓ said,

> When a person says, 'O Allāh, exalt our master Muhammad,' the real meaning of this statement is that he is entrusting the Lord ﷻ to exalt His Messenger ﷺ in a way which is befitting the sublimity of his worth, the loftiness of his degree, the eminence of his status, and everything he is worthy of.

The Shaykh ؓ also wrote,

> It is also a supplication from the one who utters it asking Allāh, the exalted, to connect him to the Prophet ﷺ. It is as if he is saying, 'O Allāh, connect me to the Prophet ﷺ!' So the invocation of *ṣalawāt* upon the Messenger of Allāh is a connection to the Prophet ﷺ. *O Allāh, make our connection with the Messenger of Allāh perpetual by allowing us to continually ask You to exalt him as You commanded us*! The act of invoking *ṣalawāt* upon the Messenger of Allāh ﷺ is therefore a supply and provision, and it is of the greatest litanies by which the servant draws near to Allāh ﷻ after the noble Qurʾān... Allāh ﷻ commanded us to invoke *ṣalawāt* upon His Messenger ﷺ so that we may take our share of the Muḥammadan Light.

It has been the practice of our pious predecessors, from the time of the Companions throughout the ages until today, to compose unique formulas of *ṣalawāt* for regular recitation. The great Companion ʿAbdullāh ibn Masʿūd ؓ used to say to people, 'Beautify your *ṣalawāt!*' He used to then give them a formula that he himself fashioned as an example of how to beautify one's *ṣalawāt* with expressions of praise of the noble Messenger of Allāh. Our master ʿAlī ibn Abī Ṭālib ؓ had his own lengthy formula which he used to teach people to recite.

1 This is a blessed authentic *ḥadīth* narrated by Imām al-Tirmidhī, Imām Aḥmad ibn Ḥanbal, Imām al-Ḥākim, and others.

2 This is a blessed authentic *ḥadīth* narrated by Imām Muslim.

The scholars of *ḥadīth* have preserved, through authentic chains of transmission, the unique formulas of *ṣalawāt* composed by several of the great Companions, Successors, and early scholars. From the generation of the Companions, we have the *ṣalawāt* of ʿAlī ibn Abī Ṭālib, ʿAbdullāh ibn Masʿūd, Anas ibn Mālik, and ʿAbdullāh ibn ʿAbbas, may Allāh be pleased with them all. From the next generation we have the *ṣalawāt* of the two great masters among the Successors, ʿAlī 'Zayn al-ʿĀbidīn' son of al-Ḥusayn, and al-Ḥasan al-Baṣrī. We also have the very long formula of the great son of Ibn ʿAbbās, ʿAlī, which the famous *ḥadīth* master al-Sakhāwī incorporated into his personal daily litanies.

Among the subsequent generations, we have the unique formula that Imām al-Shāfiʿī created and wrote in his two famous works *al-Risāla* and *Kitāb al-Umm*. Several great *ḥadīth* masters have narrated to us that after Imām al-Shāfiʿī died, he was seen in a dream, entering Paradise. As he entered Paradise, Imām al-Shāfiʿī was being honoured and welcomed as a bride is welcomed on her wedding night. When asked how he received such an immense honour, Imām al-Shāfiʿī responded that it was because of the formula of *ṣalawāt* that he wrote in his books. The great *ḥadīth* master al-Ṭabarānī, author of several of the most famous *ḥadīth* collections, wrote down his own formula which he said he received in a dream from the Messenger of Allāh ﷺ.[3]

The Knower of Allāh Shaykh Ṣāliḥ al-Jaʿfarī رضي الله عنه, who composed this present collection of *ṣalawāt*, has had similar experiences. He once saw in a dream that he was reciting the *ṣalawāt* of Shaykh Aḥmad ibn Idrīs رضي الله عنه, and the Messenger of Allāh ﷺ entered the room and said to him, 'I came to hear from you the *ṣalāt* of Ibn Idrīs.' Then the Messenger of Allāh laid down on his right side and listened, and the more that Shaykh Ṣāliḥ continued to recite, the more clearly the Messenger of Allāh appeared, and the more his light increased ﷺ. In one of his lessons in the noble Azhar Mosque he related the following dream that he saw:

> The Messenger ﷺ placed his noble hand on my face and said to me:

---

3 We also have a narration of a unique formula by ʿAbdullāh ibn ʿUmar ibn al-Khaṭṭāb but the chain suffers from some weakness. See al-Sakhāwī, *al-Qawl al-badīʿ* (Dār al-Minhāj, 2011, pp. 114-131, 489-491).

اللَّهُمَّ صَلِّ عَلَى سَيِّدِنَا مُحَمَّدٍ طِبِّ الْقُلُوبِ وَدَوَائِها وَعَافِيَةِ
الْأَبْدَانِ وَشِفَائِها وَنُورِ الْأَبْصَارِ وَضِيَائِها

Allāhumma ṣalli ʿalā sayyidinā Muḥammadin ṭibbi l-qulūbi wa
dawāʾihā wa ʿāfiyati l-abdāni wa shifāʾihā wa nūri l-abṣāri wa
ḍiyāʾihā

'O Allāh, exalt our master Muḥammad, the medicine of hearts
and their cure, the well-being of bodies and their healing, and
the light of eyes and their illumination.'

Then he commanded me to recite it.

This formula which the Messenger of Allāh encouraged Shaykh
Ṣāliḥ to recite, and which he himself recited while wiping the face of
the Shaykh with his blessed hands, is a very famous formula that has
been favoured by Muslims across the world for centuries. Similarly,
Shaykh Ṣāliḥ once saw in his dream the grandson of the Messenger
of Allāh ﷺ, al-Ḥasan ibn ʿAlī ☖, give him an *ijāza* (authorisation) to
recite a *ṣalāt* formula that was written by the famous Shaykh Aḥmad
al-Rifāʿī ☖. The purpose of such an authorisation would be to make
the recitation of the *ṣalāt* more effective for the one who receives it.
In fact it was Shaykh al-Rifāʿī himself who spoke about the benefit
of authorisations in litanies when he said, 'The authorisation is the
sword of its recipient, and the ladder through which he arrives at the
Truth.' This makes the following vision the most significant one for
us. Shaykh Ṣāliḥ wrote in one of his books,

In my dream I saw the Messenger of Allāh ﷺ in his noble
Rawḍa (in the Mosque of Medina). I greeted him and recited the Ṣalāt ʿAẓīmiyya of the great scholar and *ḥadīth*
master, the descendant of the Messenger ﷺ, Shaykh Aḥmad
ibn Idrīs ☖. I said to him, 'O Messenger of Allāh, shall I
invoke Allāh's *ṣalawāt* upon you with this formula?' He ﷺ
said, 'With it and with others too.'

I considered this to be an authorisation from him ﷺ. I
give this authorisation (in the Ṣalāt ʿAẓīmiyya in particular,
and all other formulas in general) to everyone who reads
it among the believers, as I was given it by the Messenger

of Allāh ﷺ, and I consider it to be one of the greatest of authorisations.

We therefore hope that the benefit we receive from reading the *ṣalawāt* in this book will be increased through the *baraka* (blessing) in this chain of authorisations linking us to the Messenger of Allāh ﷺ. Furthermore, Shaykh Ṣāliḥ's son and successor, Shaykh ʿAbd al-Ghanī al-Jaʿfarī, has given a general authorisation for people to recite the *ṣalawāt* of Shaykh Ṣāliḥ.

This book contains a beautiful collection of forty *ṣalawāt* written by Shaykh Ṣāliḥ al-Jaʿfarī ؓ, so that it can suffice a believer as his daily litany after the noble Qur'ān. One style of *ṣalawāt* which has been favoured by several scholars and pious men, is to incorporate praises of the Messenger of Allāh ﷺ that begin with the different letters of the Arabic alphabet. Shaykh Ṣāliḥ incorporated such an 'alphabet of praise' or 'alphabet of perfections,' as we may call it, as if to remind us that this noble Seal of the Prophets contains within him the entire range of possible perfections. It also serves to remind us that he ﷺ is the starting point of every goodness that comes to us from our Lord ﷻ, for all our blessings are attributed to us being members of his blessed ummah.

These *ṣalawāt* can be used in congregational gatherings of Remembrance, and as a personal daily litany. If used consistently on their own, they will more than suffice the believer as their daily source of spiritual growth, purification, and nourishment after the noble Qur'ān. However, I have chosen to add thirty very short *ṣalawāt* written by the author's son, Shaykh ʿAbd al-Ghanī al-Jaʿfarī, which could be recited after them to make the number seventy. Those thirty can also be read on their own at any time.

Likewise, two poems of supplication by Shaykh Ṣāliḥ are included. Shaykh Ṣāliḥ once had a beautiful vision in which he saw his teacher's teacher, Shaykh ʿAbd al-ʿĀlī son of Shaykh Aḥmad ibn Idrīs, in a dream. He asked Shaykh ʿAbd al-ʿĀlī to teach him supplications that remove difficulties and bring ease to one's affairs. The blessed shaykh pointed him to these poems which Shaykh Ṣāliḥ himself had written, and described them as 'the poems that teach *tawḥīd*,' true understanding that none deserves to be worshiped but Allāh alone. Shaykh ʿAbd al-Ghanī printed these poems along with the Forty Ṣalawāt so that they could be recited along with them both in gatherings and as part of one's daily litany. I thank Dr. Omar Mirza for the amazing work that he did in translating these two poems so that they rhyme most beautifully in the English language. The poems are so beautiful in their English rendition that I did not feel there was any need for transliterating them, as those who cannot read the Arabic can easily enjoy them just as much in English.

After the poems, the ninety-nine Names of Allāh ﷻ are included. Shaykh Ṣāliḥ recommended that people recite them twice a day, or at least once a day, to receive the blessings from each Name.

Then follows a selection of verses from the Qurʾān for protection from spiritual harm, and eight supplications of praise by Shaykh Ṣālih. In this way, this book combines in it every good. As Shaykh Ṣālih wrote,

فلازم المحامد تزد لك الموائد ، ولازم الأحزاب يفتح لك الباب ، ولازم الصلوات تمنح لك الصلات ، ولازم الحصون المنيعة تكن وأهلك عند الله وديعة ، ولازم الاستغفار تغفر لك الأوزار ، ولازم التهليل تنل السر الجليل

Be constant in praise of Allāh (*maḥāmid*), the banquets (*mawāʾid*) of divine grace will be expanded for you. ۞ Be constant in your litanies (*aḥzāb*), the door (*al-bāb*) will open for you. ۞ Be constant in your *ṣalawāt*, you will be granted your desired connections (*ṣilāt*). ۞ Be constant in reciting protective defences (*al-ḥuṣūn al-manīʿa*), you and your family will be in Allāh's safekeeping (*wadīʿa*). ۞ Be constant in seeking forgiveness (*istighfār*), you will be forgiven those things that burden your soul (*al-awzār*). ۞ Be constant in your declaration of Divine oneness (*al-tahlīl*), you will attain the sublime secret (*al-sirr al-jalīl*)

The book is finally sealed with a single special *ṣalāt* by Shaykh Ṣāliḥ, the virtue of which is explained alongside it.

To learn about the lives and teachings of the authors, see *Reassurance for the Seeker: A Biography and Translation of Ṣāliḥ al-Jaʿfarī's* al-Fawāʾid al-Jaʿfariyya, *a Commentary on Forty Prophetic Traditions* (Fons Vitae, 2013).

This work is dedicated to my daughter Rayān. I pray that she is enveloped by the blessings of these *ṣalawāt,* and that Allāh most high fill her heart with love of the Messenger of Allāh ﷺ.

The translator,
SAMER DAJANI

The Commencement of the Gathering

أَعُوذُ بِاللهِ مِنَ الشَّيْطَانِ الرَّجِيمِ

بِسْمِ اللهِ الرَّحْمٰنِ الرَّحِيمِ

الْحَمْدُ لِلّٰهِ رَبِّ الْعَالَمِينَ ۞ الرَّحْمٰنِ الرَّحِيمِ ۞ مَالِكِ يَوْمِ الدِّينِ ۞ إِيَّاكَ نَعْبُدُ وَإِيَّاكَ نَسْتَعِينُ ۞ اهْدِنَا الصِّرَاطَ الْمُسْتَقِيمَ ۞ صِرَاطَ الَّذِينَ أَنْعَمْتَ عَلَيْهِمْ غَيْرِ الْمَغْضُوبِ عَلَيْهِمْ وَلَا الضَّالِّينَ

Aᶜūdhu bi-l-Lāhi mina-sh-shayṭāni r-rajīm[4]

Bismillāhi r-Raḥmān-i r-Raḥīm, al-ḥamdu li-l-Lāhi Rabbi l-ᶜĀlamīn, ar-Raḥmān-i r-Raḥīm, māliki yawmi d-dīn, iyyāka naᶜbudu wa iyyāka nastaᶜīn, ihdina ṣ-ṣirāṭa l-mustaqīm, ṣirāṭa l-ladhīna anᶜamta ᶜalayhim, ghayri l-maghḍūbi ᶜalayhim, wala ḍ-ḍāllīn.

I seek refuge in Allāh from Satan the Outcast

﴾*In the name of Allāh, the All-Merciful the Most-Merciful. Praise be to Allāh, Lord of the Worlds, the All-Merciful the*

4 This section is recommended when doing a congregational recitation of the forty *ṣalawāt*.

Most-Merciful, King of the Day of Judgement, it is You we worship and it is You whose assistance we seek, guide us to the straight path, the path of those whom You have blessed, who have neither incurred Your anger, nor have gone astray﴾

بِسْمِ اللهِ الرَّحْمٰنِ الرَّحِيمِ

﴿إِنَّ اللهَ وَمَلَائِكَتَهُ يُصَلُّونَ عَلَى النَّبِيِّ
يَا أَيُّهَا الَّذِينَ آمَنُوا صَلُّوا عَلَيْهِ وَسَلِّمُوا تَسْلِيماً﴾

اللّٰهُمَّ صَلِّ وَسَلِّمْ عَلَى سَيِّدِنَا مُحَمَّدٍ فِي الْأَوَّلِينْ ۞ وَصَلِّ وَسَلِّمْ عَلَى سَيِّدِنَا مُحَمَّدٍ فِي الْآخِرِينْ ۞ وَصَلِّ وَسَلِّمْ عَلَى سَيِّدِنَا مُحَمَّدٍ فِي كُلِّ وَقْتٍ وَحِينْ ۞ وَصَلِّ وَسَلِّمْ عَلَى سَيِّدِنَا مُحَمَّدٍ فِي الْمَلَأِ الْأَعْلَى إِلَى يَوْمِ الدِّينْ ۞ وَصَلِّ وَسَلِّمْ عَلَى جَمِيعِ الْأَنْبِيَاءِ وَالْمُرْسَلِينْ ۞ وَعَلَى الْمَلَائِكَةِ الْمُقَرَّبِينْ ۞ وَعَلَى عِبَادِ اللهِ الصَّالِحِينْ ۞ مِنْ أَهْلِ السَّمٰوَاتِ وَأَهْلِ الْأَرَاضِينْ ۞ وَرَضِيَ اللهُ تَبَارَكَ وَتَعَالَى عَنْ سَادَتِنَا ذَوِي الْقَدْرِ الْجَلِيِّ وَالْفَخْرِ الْعَلِيِّ ۞ أَبِي بَكْرٍ وَعُمَرَ وَعُثْمَانَ وَعَلِيّ ۞ وَعَنْ سَائِرِ أَصْحَابِ رَسُولِ اللهِ أَجْمَعِينْ ۞ وَعَنِ التَّابِعِينَ لَهُمْ بِإِحْسَانٍ إِلَى يَوْمِ الدِّينْ ۞ وَاحْشُرْنَا وَارْحَمْنَا مَعَهُمْ بِرَحْمَتِكَ يَا أَرْحَمَ الرَّاحِمِينَ يَا اللهُ ۞ يَا حَيُّ يَا قَيُّومُ لَا إِلَهَ إِلَّا أَنْتَ يَا اللهُ ۞ يَا رَبَّنَا يَا وَاسِعَ الْمَغْفِرَةِ يَا أَرْحَمَ الرَّاحِمِينْ ۞ اللّٰهُمَّ آمِينْ

Bismillāhi r-Raḥmān-i r-Raḥīm

﴾*Inna l-Lāha wa malāʾikatahū yuṣallūna ʿala n-nabiyy, yā ayyuha l-ladhīna āmanū ṣallū ʿalayhi wa sallimū taslīmā*﴿

Allāhumma ṣalli wa sallim ʿalā sayyidinā Muḥammad-in fi-l-awwalīn, wa ṣalli wa sallim ʿalā sayyidinā Muḥammad-in fi-l-ākhirīn, wa ṣalli wa sallim ʿalā sayyidinā Muḥammad-in fī kulli waqtin wa ḥīn, wa ṣalli wa sallim ʿalā sayyidinā Muḥammad-in fi-l-malaʾi l-aʿlā ilā yawmi d-dīn, wa ṣalli wa sallim ʿalā jamīʿi l-anbiyāʾi wa-l-mursalīn, wa ʿala l-malāʾikati l-muqarrabīn, wa ʿalā ʿibādi l-Lāh-i ṣ-ṣāliḥīn, min ahli s-samāwāti wa ahli l-araḍīn, wa raḍiy-Allāhu tabāraka wa taʿālā ʿan sādatinā dhawi l-qadri l-jaliyyi wa-l-fakhri l-ʿalī, Abī Bakr-in wa ʿUmar-a wa ʿUthmān-a wa ʿAlī, wa ʿan sāʾiri aṣḥābi Rasūli l-Lāh-i ajmāʿīn, wa ʿani t-tābiʿīna lahum bi-iḥsānin ilā yawmi d-dīn, waḥshurnā warḥamnā maʿahum bi-raḥmatika yā arḥama r-rāḥimīna yā Allāh, yā Ḥayy-u yā Qayyūm-u lā ilāha illā anta yā Allāh, yā Rabbanā yā wāsiʿa l-maghfirati yā arḥama r-rāḥimīn, Allāhumma āmīn.

In the name of Allāh, the All-Merciful the Most-Merciful.

﴾*Allāh and His angels exalt the Prophet, O you who believe (ask Allāh to) exalt him and send greetings of peace to him in abundance*﴿

O Allāh exalt and send peace upon our master Muḥammad among the ancients. O Allāh exalt and send peace upon our master Muḥammad among the moderns. O Allāh exalt and send peace upon our master Muḥammad in every time and moment. O Allāh exalt and send peace upon our master Muḥammad among the Higher Beings until the Day of Rising. O Allāh exalt and send peace upon all the Prophets and Messengers, and the favoured angels, and righteous servants of Allāh, from amongst the inhabitants of the Heavens and the Earths. May Allāh most high be pleased with our masters whose great worth is most clear, and whose honour is most high, Abū Bakr, ʿUmar, ʿUthmān and ʿAlī, and the rest of the companions of the Messenger of Allāh, and those who followed them with excellence until the Day of Rising. O Allāh raise us with them (on that day), and shower us with mercy along with them, through Your great mercy O most merciful of the merciful, O Allāh! O Living O Sustainer, none is worthy of being worshiped but You O Allāh, O Lord whose forgiveness is most wide, O most merciful of the merciful. Amen, O Allāh!

The Forty Ṣalawāt

بِسْمِ ٱللَّهِ ٱلرَّحْمَٰنِ ٱلرَّحِيمِ

﴿إِنَّ اللهَ وَمَلائِكَتَهُ يُصَلُّونَ عَلَى النَّبِيِّ
يَا أَيُّهَا الَّذِينَ آمَنُوا صَلُّوا عَلَيْهِ وَسَلِّمُوا تَسْلِيماً﴾

اللَّهُمَّ صَلِّ عَلَى سَيِّدِنَا وَمَوْلانَا مُحَمَّدٍ وَعَلَى آلِهِ وَسَلِّمْ فِي كُلِّ
لَمْحَةٍ وَنَفَسٍ عَدَدَ مَا وَسِعَهُ عِلْمُ اللهِ

Bismillāhi r-Raḥmān-i r-Raḥīm

﴿*Inna l-Lāha wa malāʾikatahū yuṣallūna ʿala n-nabiyy, yā ayyuha l-ladhīna āmanū ṣallū ʿalayhi wa sallimū taslīmā*﴾

Allāhumma ṣalli ʿalā sayyidinā wa mawlānā Muḥammad-in wa ʿalā ālihī wa sallim fī kulli lamḥatin wa nafasin ʿadada mā wasiʿahū ʿilmu l-Lāh

In the name of Allāh the All-Merciful the Most-Merciful

﴿*Allāh and His angels exalt the Prophet, O you who believe (ask Allāh to) exalt him and send greetings of peace to him in abundance*﴾

O Allāh exalt our master and liege-lord Muḥammad and his folk and send them greetings of peace, with every glance and every breath, as many times as all that is encompassed by the knowledge of Allāh.

اللّٰهُمَّ صَلِّ عَلَى سَيِّدِنَا مُحَمَّدٍ أَفْضَلِ الْمُخْلِصِينْ ۞ وَخَاتَمِ
النَّبِيِّينْ ۞ وَسَيِّدِ وَلَدِ آدَمَ أَجْمَعِينْ ۞ صَاحِبِ التَّاجِ
وَالْمِغْفَرْ ۞ وَالْحَوْضِ وَالْكَوْثَرْ ۞ وَاللِّوَاءِ فِي الْمَحْشَرْ ۞
الْمُنِيرِ الْأَنْوَرْ ۞ وَالْخَلِيفَةِ الْأَكْبَرْ ۞ ذِي الْآيَاتِ الدَّائِمَةْ
۞ والْحُجَجِ الْقَائِمَةْ ۞ صَلَاةً تَكُونُ فَاتِحَةً لِبَابِ الرِّضَا
۞ بِعَدَدِ مَنْ بَقِيَ مِنْ خَلْقِكَ وَمَنْ مَضَى ۞ وَعَلَى آلِهِ وَسَلِّمْ

Allāhumma ṣalli ʿalā sayyidinā Muḥammad-in afḍali l-mukhliṣīn, wa-khātami n-nabiyyīn, wa-sayyidi waladi Ādam-a ajmaʿīn, ṣāḥibi t-tāji wa-l-mighfar, wa-l-ḥawḍi wa-l-kawthar, wa-l-liwāʾi fi l-maḥshar, al-munīri l-anwar, wa-l-khalīfati l-akbar, dhi l-āyāti d-dāʾima, wa-l-ḥujaji l-qāʾima, ṣalātan takūnu fātiḥatan li-bābi r-riḍā, bi-ʿadadi man baqiya min khalqika wa-man maḍā, wa ʿalā ālihī wa sallim.

O Allāh exalt our master Muḥammad the best of the sincere. The seal of the prophets. The master of all the children of Adam. Who crowned his head with a turban and chain mail. Who was gifted the Great Basin and the River Kawthar. Bearer of the standard on the Plain of Resurrection. The most luminous and illuminating. The Greatest Vicegerent. Of everlasting signs and well-established proofs. An exaltation that opens the door of Allāh's pleasure. As many times as those who have passed from among Your creation and those yet to come. And exalt his folk and send greetings of peace.

SALAT NUMBER TWO

اللّٰهُمَّ صَلِّ عَلَى سَيِّدِنَا مُحَمَّدٍ رَحْمَةِ اللهِ لِلْعَالَمِينْ ۞ وَنُورِ اللهِ الْمُبِينْ ۞ النَّاظِرِ بِكَ إِلَى مُبْدَعَاتِكْ ۞ وَالْهَادِي بِتَوْفِيقِكَ إِلَى جَنَّاتِكْ ۞ الَّذِي مَنْ بَايَعَهُ فَقَدْ بَايَعَ اللهَ ۞ وَمَنْ أَعْرَضَ عَنْهُ فَقَدْ أَعْرَضَ عَنِ اللهِ ۞ رَئِيسِ حِزْبِ اللهِ ۞ وَمَوْضِعِ عِنَايَةِ اللهِ ۞ وَعَلَى آلِهِ وَسَلِّمْ

Allāhumma ṣalli ʿalā sayyidinā Muḥammad-in raḥmati l-Lāhi li-l-ʿālamīn, wa nuri l-Lāhi l-mubīn, an-nāẓiri bika ilā mubdaʿātik, wa-l-hādī bitawfīqika ilā jannātik, alladhī man bāyaʿahū fa-qad bāyaʿa l-Lāh, wa-man aʿraḍa ʿanhu fa-qad aʿraḍa ʿani-l-Lāh, raʾīsi ḥizbi l-Lāh, wa-mawḍiʿi ʿināyati l-Lāh, wa ʿalā ālihī wa sallim.

O Allāh exalt our master Muḥammad, Allāh's mercy to all the worlds. Allāh's clear light. Who gazes at Your creations through You, and guides to Your Gardens with Your help. The one to whom a pledge of allegiance is a pledge of allegiance to Allāh, and who, those who turn away from him turn away from Allāh. The chief of the Party of Allāh, who is always surrounded by the care of Allāh. And exalt his folk and send greetings of peace.

SALAT NUMBER THREE

اللَّهُمَّ صَلِّ عَلَى سَيِّدِنَا مُحَمَّدٍ مَدِينَةِ الْعِلْمِ الْكُبْرَى ۞ وَجَدِّ
الْحَسَنَيْنِ وَوَالِدِ الزَّهْرَا ۞ مَنْ طَابَتْ بِهِ طَيْبَةُ وَأَهْلُهَا ۞
وَذَهَبَ بِهِ حَرُّهَا ۞ وَثَبَتَ فَضْلُهَا ۞ ذِي الرَّوَائِحِ الْمِسْكِيَّةِ
۞ وَالثِّيَابِ الْخُضْرِ السُّنْدُسِيَّةِ ۞ مُقَسِّمُ نَعِيمِ الْجِنَانِ فَهُوَ
الْقَاسِمْ ۞ الَّذِي يُحْشَرُ النَّاسُ عَلَى قَدَمِهِ فَهُوَ الْحَاشِرْ ۞
نَبِيُّ الْإِنَابَةِ فَهُوَ الْمُنِيبْ ۞ وَصَاحِبُ الْمَوَدَّةِ فَهُوَ الْحَبِيبْ ۞
أَحْمَدُكَ الْحَامِدْ ۞ وَمُحَمَّدُكَ الْمَاجِدْ ۞ عَبْدُ اللهِ وَرَسُولُهُ
الْمُتَوَكِّلُ عَلَى الْمَلِكِ الْجَلِيلْ ۞ النَّبِيُّ الْأُمِّيُّ السَّيِّدُ الْإِكْلِيلْ
۞ صَلَاةً نَنَالُ بِهَا مِنَ الْعِلْمِ أَنْفَعَهْ ۞ وَمِنَ الرِّزْقِ أَوْسَعَهْ
۞ وَمِنَ الْعَمَلِ أَدْوَمَهْ ۞ وَعَلَى آلِهِ وَسَلِّمْ

Allāhumma ṣalli ʿalā sayyidinā Muḥammad-in madīnati l-ʿilmi l-kubrā, wa jaddi l-ḥasanayni wa-wālidi z-Zahrā, man ṭābat bihī Ṭayba-tu wa ahluhā, wa dhahaba bihī ḥarruhā, wa thabata faḍluhā, dhi r-rawāʾiḥi l-miskiyya, wa-th-thiyābi l-khuḍri s-sundusiyya, muqassimu naʿīmi l-jināni fa-huwa l-qāsim, alladhī yuḥsharu n-nāsu ʿalā qadamihī fa-huwa l-ḥāshir, nabiyyu l-inābati fa-huwa l-munīb, wa ṣāḥibu l-mawaddati fa-huwa l-ḥabīb, Aḥmad-uka l-ḥāmid, wa Muḥammad-uka l-mājid, ʿAbdullāh-i wa-rasūluhu l-mutawakkilu ʿala l-maliki l-jalīl, an-nabiyyu l-ummiyyu s-sayyidu l-iklīl, ṣalātan nanālu bihā mina l-ʿilmi anfaʿah, wa mina r-rizqi awsaʿah, wa mina l-ʿamali adwamah, wa ʿalā ālihī wa sallim.

O Allāh exalt our master Muḥammad, the Great City of Knowledge. The Grandfather of al-Ḥasan and al-Ḥusayn, and the father of Fāṭima the Radiant. The one who brought goodness to Ṭayba and its inhabitants, and removed from it its plague, and gave it everlasting virtue. Who smelled of musk, and who will be dressed in the afterlife in silken green robes. The distributor of the bliss of the Gardens, for he is the Distributor (al-Qāsim). Behind whom the people will be resurrected and gathered, for he is the Gatherer (al-Ḥāshir). The Prophet of Attachment to Allāh, for he is the Attached One. The recipient of Your love, for he is the Beloved. Your Aḥmad, the greatest in praise of You. Your Muḥammad, most praised and glorious. The servant of Allāh and His Messenger, who relies upon the Most Majestic King. The Unlettered Prophet, the Master, the Laurel Wreath. An exaltation by which we gain the most beneficial of knowledge, and the most expansive sustenance, and the most constant pious works. And exalt his folk and send greetings of peace.

SALAT NUMBER FOUR

اللّٰهُمَّ صَلِّ عَلَى سَيِّدِنَا مُحَمَّدٍ صَاحِبِ النَّصْرِ عَظِيمِ الْأَجْرْ
۞ الَّذِي مِنْ نُورِهِ الشَّمْسُ وَالْبَدْرْ ۞ الْوَجِيهِ عِنْدَكْ ۞
الَّذِي أَنْزَلْتَ لَهُ الْمَلَائِكَةَ يَوْمَ بَدْرْ ۞ مُجَابِ الدُّعَاءْ ۞
ذِي النَّصْرِ عَلَى الْأَعْدَاءْ ۞ الْمُؤَيَّدِ بِالثَّبَاتْ ۞ وَالدَّاعِي إِلَى
الْحَسَنَاتْ ۞ ذِي الْفَيْضِ الرَّاوِي وَالْفَضْلِ الْمُشْتَهَرْ ۞
وَالْعِزِّ بِاللّٰهِ وِالصِّدْقِ فِي الْخَبَرْ ۞ النَّبِيِّ الرَّءُوفْ ۞ النَّبِيِّ
الْعَطُوفْ ۞ النَّبِيِّ الشَّفُوقْ ۞ النَّبِيِّ الرَّحِيمْ ۞ ذِي السِّرِّ
السَّارِي ۞ وَالثَّوَابِ الْجَارِي ۞ الَّذِي نَارَتْ بِهِ الْأَكْوَانْ
۞ وَتَشَرَّفَتْ بِقُدُومِهِ الْبُلْدَانْ ۞ أَحْمَدُ الْخَلَائِقِ وَصَفْوَةُ
الْبَارِي ۞ بِعَدَدِ كُلِّ كَاتِبٍ وَقَارِي ۞ وَعَلَى آلِهِ وَسَلِّمْ ۞
تَسْلِيماً نَسْلَمُ بِهِ مِنَ الْآفَاتْ ۞ فِي الْمَحْيَا وَالْمَمَاتْ

Allāhumma ṣalli ʿalā sayyidinā Muḥammad-in ṣāhibi n-naṣri ʿaẓīmi l-ajr, alladhī min-nūrihi sh-shamsu wa-l-badr, al-wajīhi ʿindak, alladhī anzalta lahu l-malāʾikata yawma Badr, mujābi d-duʿāʾ, dhi n-naṣri ʿala l-aʿdāʾ, al-muʾayyadi bi-th-thabāt, wa-d-dāʿī ila l-ḥasanāt, dhil fayḍi r-rāwī wa-l-faḍli l-mushtahar, wa-l-ʿizzi bil-Lāhi wa-ṣ-ṣidqi fi l-khabar, an-nabiyyi r-raʾūf, an-nabiyyi l-ʿaṭūf, an-nabiyyi-sh-shafūq, an-nabiyyi-r-raḥīm, dhi s-sirri s-sārī, wa-th-thawābi l-jārī, alladhī nārat bihi l-akwān, wa-tasharrafat bi-qudūmihi l-buldān, aḥmadu l-khalāʾiqi wa ṣafwatu l-Bārī, biʿadadi kulli kātibin wa qārī, wa-ʿalā ālihī wa sallim, taslīman naslamu bihī mina l-āfāt, fi l-maḥyā wa-l-mamāt.

O Allāh exalt our master Muḥammad, the victorious, who will receive the greatest reward. Whose light exceeds that of the sun and the full moon. Most eminent in Your sight. To whom you sent the angels at the Battle of Badr. Whose supplications are answered, and whose enemies are vanquished. Who is supported with firmness, and who guides to good deeds. Whose flood of blessings quenches all, and whose virtue is known to all. Whose honour comes through Allāh, and whose speech is truthful. The Compassionate Prophet. The Caring Prophet. The Affectionate Prophet. The Merciful Prophet. Of flowing secret and continuous reward. Through whom the universe was illuminated, and by whose coming the lands were honoured. The most praising among Your creation, the Chosen One of the Creator. As many times as the number of every writer and every reader, and exalt his folk. And send greetings of peace in abundance, through the blessings of which we are secure from every harm, in life and in death.

اللّٰهُمَّ صَلِّ عَلَى سَيِّدِنَا مُحَمَّدْ ۞ نُورِكَ الْمَاحِي بِضِيَائِهِ
ظَلَامَ الشِّرْكْ ۞ وَنَبِيِّكَ الَّذِي نَبَّأْتَهُ قَبْلَ خَلْقِ كُلِّ فَرْدْ ۞
وَرَسُولِكَ الَّذِي أَرْسَلْتَهُ لِكُلِّ مَا سِوَاكْ ۞ فَقَامَ إِلَيْكَ وَدَعَاكْ
۞ وَأَرْشَدَ إِلَى صِرَاطِكَ الْمُسْتَقِيمْ ۞ وَجَاهَدَ فِي سَبِيلِكَ
لِإِعْلَاءِ دِينِكْ ۞ وَجَادَلَ أَعْدَاءَكَ وَأَقَامَ الْحُجَّةَ عَلَيْهِمْ
۞ فَكَانَ لَكَ كَمَا كُنْتَ لَهْ ۞ وَكَانَ بِالْمُؤْمِنِينَ كَمَا أَرَدْتَ
مِنْهْ ۞ وَبِالْكَافِرِينَ كَمَا أَمَرْتَهْ ۞ مَنْ كَانَ خُلُقُهُ الْقُرْآنْ
۞ وَجَلِيسُهُ الرَّحْمٰنْ ۞ ذِي الْقَلْبِ الْخَشُوعْ ۞ وَالذِّكْرِ
الْمَرْفُوعْ ۞ صَلَاةً أَنَالُ بِبَرَكَتِهَا حُسْنَ الْخِتَامْ ۞ وَثَوَابَ
الْقَبُولِ وَالْإِكْرَامْ ۞ وَعَلَى آلِهِ وَسَلِّمْ

Allāhumma ṣalli ʿalā sayyidinā Muḥammad, nūrika l-māḥī bi-ḍiyāʾihī ẓalāma sh-shirk, wa nabiyyika l-ladhī nabbaʾtahū qabla khalqi kulli fard, wa rasūlika l-ladhī arsaltahū li-kulli mā siwāk, fa-qāma ilayka wa daʿāk, wa arshada ilā ṣirāṭika l-mustaqīm, wa jāhada fī sabīlika li-iʿlāʾi dīnik, wa jādala aʿdāʾaka wa-aqāma l-ḥujjata ʿalayhim, fa-kāna laka kamā kunta lah, wa-kāna bi-l-muʾminīna kamā aradta minh, wa bi-l-kāfirīna kamā amartah, man kāna khuluquhu l-Qurʾān, wa jalīsuhu r-Raḥmān, dhi l-qalbi l-khashūʿ, wa-dh-dhikri l-marfūʿ, ṣalātan anālu bi-barakatihā ḥusna l-khitām, wa thawāba l-qabūli wa-l-ikrām, wa ʿalā ālihī wa sallim.

O Allāh exalt our master Muḥammad. Your light whose illumination erases the darkness of polytheism. Your Prophet whom You elevated and taught before the creation of all else. Your Messenger whom You sent to all other than You. So he rose for Your sake, and called out to You! And guided to Your straight path. And strived to elevate Your religion. And debated Your enemies and put forth Your proof against them. He was for You as You were for him, and with the believers as You wanted him to be, and with the disbelievers as You commanded him to be. Whose character was the personification of the Qurʾān, and whose sitting-companion was the All-Merciful. Whose heart was submissive to You, and whose mention was raised by You. An exaltation by the blessing of which my life is sealed with goodness, and I am rewarded with Your acceptance and honouring. And exalt his folk and send greetings of peace.

SALAT NUMBER SIX

اللّٰهُمَّ صَلِّ عَلَى سَيِّدِنَا مُحَمَّدٍ طَاهِرِ الْفُؤَادْ ۞ كَثِيرِ الْوِدَادِ
لِرَبِّ الْعِبَادْ ۞ ذِي الْكَلِمَاتِ الْجَامِعَةْ ۞ وَالْعُلُومِ النَّافِعَةْ
۞ وَالْأَنْوَارِ السَّاطِعَةْ ۞ بَشِيرِكَ الْمُبَشِّرْ ۞ وَنَذِيرِكَ
الْمُنْذِرْ ۞ وَسِرَاجِكَ الْمُنِيرْ ۞ أَفْلَحِ الْمُفْلِحِينْ ۞
وَأَصْلَحِ الْمُصْلِحِينْ ۞ وَعَلَى آلِهِ وَسَلِّمْ

Allāhumma ṣalli ʿalā sayyidinā Muḥammad-in ṭāhiri l-fuʾād, kathīri l-widādi li-rabbi l-ʿibād, dhi l-kalimāti l-jāmiʿa, wa-l-ʿulūmi n-nāfiʿa, wa-l-anwāri s-sāṭiʿa, bashīrika l-mubash-shir, wa nadhīrika l-mundhir, wa sirājika l-munīr, aflaḥi l-mufliḥīn, wa aṣlaḥi l-muṣliḥīn, wa ʿalā ālihī wa sallim.

O Allāh exalt our master Muḥammad the pure-hearted, who greatly loved You. Whose words were concise and laden with meaning, and who taught the most beneficial branches of knowledge. Whose lights shine forth. The one You sent as a giver of glad tidings and a warner. Your illuminating sun. The most successful of all who are successful, and the greatest of doers of good. And exalt his folk and send greetings of peace.

اللّٰهُمَّ صَلِّ عَلَى سَيِّدِنَا مُحَمَّدْ ۞ الَّذِي فِرَارُ النَّاسِ إِلَيْهِ
عِنْدَ الْمَخَاوِفِ وَيَوْمَ الْقِيَامَةْ ۞ صَاحِبِ التَّاجِ وَالْمِعْرَاجِ
وَالْعَلَامَةْ ۞ نَبِيِّكَ الشَّافِي لِلْقُلُوبِ بِحِكْمَتِهْ ۞ وَأَمِينِكَ
الَّذِي شَهِدَتِ الْأَعْدَاءُ بِجُودِهِ وَفِطْنَتِهْ ۞ ذِي الْعَدْلِ الرَّبَّانِي
۞ وَالْفَيْضِ الرَّحْمَانِي ۞ وَعَلَى آلِهِ وَسَلِّمْ ۞ وَنَسْأَلُكَ
اللّٰهُمَّ فُتُوحَ الْعَارِفِينْ ۞ وَإِخْلَاصَ الْمُوقِنِينْ ۞ وَتَوَكُّلَ
الزَّاهِدِينْ

Allāhumma ṣalli ʿalā sayyidinā Muḥammad, alladhī firāru n-nāsi ilayhi ʿinda l-makhāwifi wa yawma l-qiyāma, ṣāḥibi t-tāji wa-l-miʿrāji wa-l-ʿalāma, nabiyyika sh-shāfī li-l-qulūbi bi-ḥikmatih, wa amīnika l-ladhī shahidati l-aʿdāʾu bi-jūdihī wa-fiṭnatih, dhi l-ʿadli r-rabbānī, wa-l-fayḍi r-raḥmānī, wa ʿalā ālihī wa sallim, wa nasʾaluka l-Lāhumma futūḥa l-ʿārifīn, wa ikhlāṣa l-mūqinīn, wa tawakkula z-zāhidīn.

O Allāh exalt our Master Muḥammad, to whom people escape in times of fright and on the Day of Resurrection. Who crowned his head with a turban, ascended the heavens, and possessed a distinguishing mark of prophethood. Your Prophet who heals hearts with his wisdom. Your Trustworthy One whose enemies attested to his generosity and intelligence. Who ruled with Divine Justice and was a flood of Divine Mercy. And exalt his folk and send greetings of peace. And we ask you O Allāh for the illuminations of the Knowers of Allāh, the sincerity of the people of certainty, and the reliance of the ascetics.

SALAT NUMBER EIGHT

اللّٰهُمَّ صَلِّ عَلَى سَيِّدِنَا مُحَمَّدٍ بَدْرِ الْبُدُورْ ۞ وَبَابِ الْفَرَجِ وَالسُّرُورْ ۞ دَعْوَةِ أَبِيهِ إِبْرَاهِيمْ ۞ وَمَظْهَرِ كَرَمِ الرَّبِّ الْكَرِيمْ ۞ ذِي الْمَدَدِ الْمُفَاضِ عَلَى أَهْلِ وِدَادِهْ ۞ وَالْعِلْمِ الْمَشْهُورِ لَدَى أَهْلِ إِسْعَادِهْ ۞ أَلِفِ الْأُلْفَةْ ۞ الَّتِي أَلَّفَ اللهُ بِهَا بَيْنَ الْقُلُوبِ الْمُتَنَافِرَةْ ۞ وَبَاءِ الْبَرَكَةْ ۞ الَّتِي عَمَّتْ بِالْخَيْرَاتِ الْمُتَكَاثِرَةْ ۞ وَعَلَى أَصْحَابِهِ وَذُرِّيَّتِهِ وَأَهْلِ بَيْتِهْ ۞ وَسَلِّمْ تَسْلِيماً كَثِيرَا ۞ نَسْلَمُ بِهِ مِنْ كُلِّ مَا نَخَافْ ۞ يَا لَطِيفَ الْأَلْطَافْ

Allāhumma ṣalli ʿalā sayyidinā Muḥammad-in badri l-budūr, wa bābi l-faraji wa-s-surūr, daʿwati abīhi Ibrāhīm, wa maẓhari karami r-Rabb-i l-karīm, dhi l-madadi l-mufāḍi ʿalā ahli widādih, wa-l-ʿilmi l-mash-hūri ladā ahli isʿādih, alifi l-ulfa, allatī allafa l-Lāhu bihā bayna l-qulūbi l-mutanāfira, wa bāʾi l-baraka, allatī ʿammat bi-l-khayrāti l-mutakāthira, wa ʿalā aṣḥābihī wa dhurriyyatihī wa ahli baytih, wa sallim taslīman kathīrā, naslamu bihī min kulli mā nakhāf, yā laṭīfa l-alṭāf.

O Allāh exalt our master Muḥammad the most beautiful of full moons, the gate to relief and joy. The answer to the prayer of his ancestor Abraham, and the manifestation of the generosity of the Most Generous Lord. Whose support overflows unto those who love him. Whose knowledge is acquired by those whose joy is in him. The *alif* of *ulfa* (harmony) which Allāh put in hearts that had been in discord, and the *bāʾ* of *baraka* (blessings) that covered all with great good. And exalt his Companions, progeny, and the People of his Household. And send them many greetings of peace through the blessings of

which we are kept safe from all that which we fear,
O Most Kind and Subtle One, of kind and subtle care.

SALAT NUMBER NINE

اللّٰهُمَّ صَلِّ عَلَى النَّبِيِّ الصَّادِقْ ۞ سَيِّدِنَا مُحَمَّدٍ خِيرَةِ اللهِ مِنَ الخَلَائِقْ ۞ الرَّشِيدِ الْمُرْشِدْ ۞ الْمُقَرِّبِ لِلْجَنَّةِ وِمِنَ النَّارِ مُبْعِدْ ۞ الْأَوَّلِ الخَاتِمْ ۞ وَالخَلِيفَةِ الحَاكِمْ ۞ الَّذِي اخْتَرْتَ لَهُ قَبْلَ أَنْ يَخْتَارْ ۞ وَسَمَّيْتَهُ الحَبِيبَ الْمُخْتَارْ ۞ الَّذِي أَخَذْتَ عَلَى أَنْبِيَائِكَ مِيثَاقاً بِنَصْرِهْ ۞ وَشَرَّفْتَ أُمَّتَهُ بِلَيْلَةِ قَدْرِهْ ۞ جِيمِ الجَمَالِ الْبَاهِرْ ۞ وَحَاءِ الحِلْمِ الْغَافِرْ ۞ وَعَلَى آلِهِ وَسَلِّمْ

Allāhumma ṣalli ʿala n-nabiyyi ṣ-ṣādiq, sayyidinā Muḥammad-in khīrati l-Lāhi mina l-khalāʾiq, ar-rashīdi l-murshid, al-muqarribi li-l-jannati wa-mina n-nāri mubʿid, al-awwali l-khātim, wa-l-khalīfati-l ḥākim, alladhī kh-tarta lahū qabla an yakhtār, wa sammaytahu l-ḥabība l-mukhtār, alladhī akhadhta ʿalā anbiyāʾika mīthāqan bi-naṣrih, wa sharrafta ummatahū bi laylati qadrih, jīmi l-jamāli l-bāhir, wa ḥāʾi l-ḥilmi l-ghāfir, wa ʿalā ālihī wa sallim.

O Allāh exalt the truthful Prophet. Our master Muḥammad, Allāh's Chosen One from among all creation. The guide, the rightly-guided. Who brings people closer to Paradise and pushes them away from the Fire. The first and the seal, and the ruling vicegerent. For whom You chose before he chose, and You called him the Beloved, the Chosen One. The one for whose sake You took a pledge from Your prophets to give him victory, and whose community You honoured with the Night of his Honour. The *jīm* of astounding *jamāl* (beauty), and *ḥāʾ* of forgiving *ḥilm* (forbearance).

اللّٰهُمَّ صَلِّ عَلَى سَيِّدِنَا مُحَمَّدْ ۞ الْعَاقِبِ الذَّكِيِّ الطَّاهِرْ
۞ الْمُذَكِّرِ الذَّاكِرْ ۞ الَّذِي سَطَعَتْ أَنْوَارُهْ ۞ وَحَظِيَتْ
بِالشَّفَاعَةِ زُوَّارُهْ ۞ أَكْبَرِ آيَةٍ وَأَعْظَمِ نِعْمَةْ ۞ ذِي النَّفْسِ
الْكَامِلَةِ الْمُكَمَّلَةْ ۞ والرُّوحِ الْعَالِمَةِ الْمُعَلِّمَةْ ۞ نَبِيِّ الْعِلْمِ
وَالتَّعْلِيمْ ۞ وَالتَّحْلِيلِ وَالتَّحْرِيمْ ۞ مُطَهِّرِ النُّفُوسْ ۞
بِالْخُطَبِ وَالدُّرُوسْ ۞ رَئِيسِ حِزْبِ اللهْ ۞ وَعَدُوِّ حِزْبِ
مَا سِوَاهْ ۞ الَّذِي بِسُلْطَانِهِ الْأَعْظَمِ جَمْعُ الْكُفْرِ انْدَثَرْ ۞
صَاحِبِ الطَّيِّبَيْنِ أَبِي بَكْرٍ وَعُمَرْ ۞ تَاءِ التَّوْبَةِ الصَّادِقَةْ
۞ الَّتِي بِهَا يَتُوبُ اللهُ عَلَى التَّائِبِينْ ۞ وَثَاءِ الثَّوَابِ الْعَظِيمْ
۞ الَّذِي يَمُنُّ اللهُ بِهِ عَلَى الطَّائِعِينْ ۞ وَعَلَى آلِهِ وَسَلِّمْ ۞
وَأَدِمْ عِزَّنَا وَإِكْرَامَنَا بِدَوَامِ عِزِّكَ يَا عَزِيزُ يَا كَرِيمْ

Allāhumma ṣalli ʿalā sayyidinā Muḥammad, al-ʿāqibi dh-dhakiyyi ṭ-ṭāhir, al-mudhakkiri dh-dhākir, alladhī saṭaʿat anwāruh, wa ḥaẓiyat bi-sh-shafāʿati zuwwāruh, akbari āyatin wa aʿẓami niʿma, dhi-n-nafsi l-kāmilati l-mukammala, wa-r-rūḥi l-ʿālimati l-muʿallima, nabiyyi l-ʿilmi wa-t-taʿlīm, wa-t-taḥlīli wa-t-taḥrīm, muṭahhiri n-nufūs, bi-l-khuṭabi wa-d-durūs, raʾīsi ḥizbi l-Lāh, wa ʿaduwwi ḥizbi mā siwāh, alladhī bi-ṣulṭānihi l-aʿẓam jamʿu l-kufri n-dathar, ṣāḥibi ṭ-ṭayyibayni Abī Bakr-in wa ʿUmar, tāʾi t-tawbati ṣ-ṣādiqa, allatī bihā yatūbu l-Lāhu ʿala t-tāʾibīn, wa thāʾi th-thawābi l-ʿaẓīm, alladhī yamunnu l-Lāhu bihī ʿala ṭ-ṭāʾiʿīn, wa ʿalā ālihī wa sallim, wa adim ʿizzanā wa ikrāmanā bi-dawāmi ʿizzika yā ʿAzīz-u yā Karīm.

O Allāh exalt our master Muḥammad. The last of the prophets, the intelligent, the pure. The reminder who was in constant remembrance of You. Whose lights shone forth, and whose visitors gained his intercession. The grandest sign and greatest blessing. Whose soul is complete and perfected, and whose spirit is a most knowledgeable teacher. The Prophet of knowledge and teaching, and guidance to what is permissible and what is forbidden. The purifier of souls through speeches and lessons. The chief of the Party of Allāh, and the enemy of the party of what is other than Him. By whose great power the horde of falsehood disappeared. Who was accompanied by the pure ones Abū Bakr and ʿUmar. The *tāʾ* of sincere *tawba* (repentance), through which Allāh turns to those who turn to Him. The *thāʾ* of great *thawāb* (reward) which Allāh gifts to those who obey Him. And exalt his folk and send greetings of peace. And keep our honour and dignity perpetual with Your lasting Honour, O Most Honourable and Most Generous.

اللّٰهُمَّ صَلِّ عَلَى الشَّفِيعِ الْمُشَفَّعْ ❁ سَيِّدِنَا مُحَمَّدِ بِنِ عَبْدِ
اللهِ ❁ صَلَاةً يَعْقُبُهَا نَصْرٌ مِنَ اللهِ ❁ وَفَتْحٌ مِنَ اللهِ ❁
وَبَرَكَةٌ مِنَ اللهِ ❁ وَنُورٌ مِنَ اللهِ ❁ وَفَرَجٌ مِنَ اللهِ ❁
وَعِلْمٌ مِنَ اللهِ ❁ وَدِفَاعٌ مِنَ اللهِ ❁ وَقُرْبٌ مِنَ اللهِ ❁
وَإِلْهَامٌ مِنَ اللهِ ❁ وَبُرْهَانٌ مِنَ اللهِ ❁ وَأَمَانٌ مِنَ اللهِ ❁
وَتَخْفِيفٌ مِنَ اللهِ ❁ وَتَأْيِيدٌ مِنَ اللهِ ❁ وَثَبَاتٌ مِنَ اللهِ
❁ وَضِيَاءٌ مِنَ اللهِ ❁ وَرِضْوَانٌ مِنَ اللهِ ❁ وَعَفْوٌ مِنَ اللهِ
❁ وَسَتْرٌ مِنَ اللهِ ❁ وَ رِزْقٌ مِنَ اللهِ ❁ وَغِنىً مِنَ اللهِ
❁ وَعَافِيَةٌ مِنَ اللهِ ❁ وَجَلَالٌ مِنَ اللهِ ❁ وَهَيْبَةٌ مِنَ اللهِ
❁ وَتَوْفِيقٌ مِنَ اللهِ ❁ وَسَلَامَةٌ مِنَ اللهِ ❁ بِجَاهِ حَبِيبِ
اللهِ وَرَسُولِ اللهِ وَنَبِيِّ اللهِ ❁ ذِي الْخُلُقِ الْعَظِيمِ ❁ وَالْجَاهِ
الْعَظِيمِ ❁ وَالْفَضْلِ الْعَمِيمِ ❁ وَالْقَلْبِ الرَّحِيمِ ❁ وَعَلَى
آلِهِ وَسَلِّمْ

Allāhumma ṣalli ʿala sh-shafīʿi l-mushaffaʿ, sayyidinā Muḥammad-in ibni ʿAbdillāh, ṣalātan yaʿqubuhā naṣrun min-Allāh, wa fatḥun min-Allāh, wa barakatun min-Allāh, wa nūrun min-Allāh, wa farajun min-Allāh, wa ʿilmun min-Allāh, wa difāʿun min-Allāh, wa qurbun min-Allāh, wa ilhāmun min-Allāh, wa burhānun min-Allāh, wa amānun min-Allāh, wa takhfīfun min-Allāh, wa taʾyīdun min-Allāh, wa thabātun min-Allāh, wa ḍiyāʾun min-Allāh, wa riḍwānun min-Allāh, wa ʿafwun min-Allāh, wa satrun min-Allāh, wa rizqun min-Allāh, wa ghinan min-Allāh, wa ʿāfiyatun min-Allāh, wa jalālun min-

Allāh, wa haybatun min-Allāh, wa tawfīqun min-Allāh, wa salāmatun min-Allāh, bi-jāhi ḥabībi l-Lāhi wa rasūli l-Lāhi, wa nabiyyi l-Lāh, dhi l-khuluqi l-ʿaẓīm, wa-l-jāhi l-ʿaẓīm, wa-l-faḍli l-ʿamīm, wa-l-qalbi r-raḥīm, wa ʿalā ālihī wa sallim.

O Allāh exalt the best intercessor, who will be told to intercede by Allāh. Our master Muḥammad son of ʿAbdullāh. An exaltation through the blessings of which I gain victory from Allāh, and openings from Allāh, and blessings from Allāh, and light from Allāh, and relief from Allāh, and knowledge from Allāh, and defence from Allāh, and proximity to Allāh, and inspiration from Allāh, and strong evidence from Allāh, and safety from Allāh, and ease from Allāh, and support from Allāh, and firmness through Allāh, and illumination from Allāh, and the pleasure of Allāh, and pardon from Allāh, and the covering of faults from Allāh, and sustenance from Allāh, and sufficiency through Allāh, and well-being from Allāh, and majesty from Allāh, and awe-inspiring presence from Allāh, and help from Allāh, and security from Allāh. Through the rank of the Beloved of Allāh, the Messenger of Allāh, the Prophet of Allāh. Of character most great, eminence most great, all-encompassing grace, and a most merciful heart. And exalt his folk and send greetings of peace.

SALAT NUMBER TWELVE

اللّٰهُمَّ صَلِّ عَلَى سَيِّدِنَا مُحَمَّدٍ نَبِيِّ السَّلَامَةِ وَالْأَمْنْ ۞
وَالدِّعَايَةِ إِلَى الْحَقّ ۞ ذِي الْمِلَّةِ الْحَنِيفِيَّةْ ۞ وَالسِّيرَةِ
الْمَرْضِيَّةْ ۞ الْمُتَلَذِّذِ بِسَمَاعِ مَا لَمْ نَسْمَعْ ۞ وَالْمُعْتَبِرِ
بِرُؤْيَةِ مَا لَا نَرَى ۞ السَّامِعِ بِالسَّمِيعْ ۞ وَالْمُبْصِرِ بِالْبَصِيرْ
۞ الَّذِي إِذَا أَعْطَى كُنْتَ أَنْتَ الْمُعْطِي ۞ وَهُوَ الْقَاسِمْ
۞ سَيِّدِنَا الْمُجِيرِ أَبِي الْقَاسِمْ ۞ دَالِ الدِّينِ الْحَنِيفْ ۞
وَذَالِ الذَّكَاءِ الْمَوْهُوبِ لَهُ مِنَ الْخَبِيرِ اللَّطِيفْ ۞ وَعَلَى
آلِهِ وَسَلِّمْ وَبَارِكْ ۞ وَهَبْ لَنَا مِنْكَ مَا تُحِبُّهُ وَتَرْضَاهْ ۞
وَارْزُقْنَا الْإِخْلَاصَ فِيهْ ۞ بِجَاهِ أَفْضَلِ شَفِيعٍ عِنْدَكَ يَوْمَ
الْقِيَامَةِ تَرْتَضِيهْ

Allāhumma ṣalli ʿalā sayyidinā Muḥammad-in, nabiyyi s-salāmati wa-l-amn, wa-d-diʿāyati ila l-ḥaqq, dhi l-millati l-ḥanīfiyya, wa-s-sīrati l-marḍiyya, al-mutaladh-dhi-dhi bi-samāʿi mā lam nasmaʿ, wa-l-muʿtabiri bi-ruʾyati mā lā narā, as-sāmiʿi bi-s-Samīʿ, wa-l-mubṣiri bi-l-Baṣīr, alladhī idhā aʿṭā kunta anta l-muʿṭī, wa huwa l-qāsim, sayyidina l-mujīri Abi l-Qāsim, dāli d-dīni l-ḥanīf, wa dhāli dh-dhakāʾi l-mawhūbi lahū mina l-Khabīr-i l-Laṭīf, wa ʿalā ālihī wa sallim wa bārik, wa hab lanā minka mā tuḥibbuhū wa tarḍāh, wa-r-zuqna l-ikhlāṣa fīh, bi-jāhi afḍali shafīʿin ʿindaka yawma l-qiyāmati tartaḍīh.

O Allāh exalt our master Muḥammad the Prophet of safety and security, and invitation to the Truth. Who came with the primordial monotheistic way, and the most pleasing example. Who found pleasure in hearing what we could not hear, and who took lesson from seeing what we could not see. Who heard through the All-Hearing and saw through the All-Seeing. The one who, when he gave, it was You who gave. And he was the Distributor (*al-Qāsim*). Our master, the giver of refuge, Abu l-Qāsim. The *dāl* of the primordial *dīn* (religion), and the *dhāl* of the *dhakā*ʾ (intelligence) that he was gifted from the Most Knowing, the Subtle. And exalt his folk and send blessings and greetings of peace. And grant us from You that which You love and that which pleases You, and grant us sincerity in it. By the eminent rank of the best intercessor in Your sight, whose intercession You will be pleased with on the Day of Resurrection.

اللّٰهُمَّ صَلِّ عَلَى سَيِّدِنَا مُحَمَّدْ ۞ الَّذِي خَضَعَ لِهَيْبَةِ جَلالِهِ
كُلُّ مُعَانِدْ ۞ وَأَطْفَأَ اللهُ بِسِرِّ نُورِهِ نَارَ كُلِّ عَدُوٍّ وَحَاسِدْ
۞ الَّذِي جَاءَ نَعْتُهُ فِي كُتُبِ السَّابِقِينْ ۞ وَعَمَّتْ
بَرَكَتُهُ الْأَوَّلِينَ وَالْآخِرِينْ ۞ الْغَيْثِ الْمِدْرَارْ ۞ الَّذِي
هَطَلَتْ نَفَائِسُ دُرِّهِ عَلَى أَرْضِ الْقُلُوبْ ۞ فَاهْتَزَّتْ وَرَبَتْ
وَاطْمَأَنَّتْ لِرَبِّهَا ۞ فَرَأَتِ الْحَقَّ ظَاهِراً فَاتَّبَعَتْهْ ۞ وَالْبَاطِلَ
رِجْساً فَهَجَرَتْهْ ۞ عَيْنِ الْعُلُومِ اللَّدُنِّيَّةْ ۞ وَغَيْنِ الْغَيْرَةِ
لِانْتِهَاكِ الْحُرُمَاتِ الْإِلٰهِيَّةْ ۞ وَعَلَى آلِهِ وَسَلِّمْ ۞ وَأَدِمْ
بَرَكَاتِكَ عَلَيْهْ ۞ وَعَلَى أَهْلِ بَيْتِهِ الَّذِينَ أَذْهَبْتَ عَنْهُمُ
الرِّجْسَ وَطَهَّرْتَهُمْ تَطْهِيرَا

Allāhumma ṣalli ʿalā sayyidinā Muḥammad, alladhī khaḍaʿa li-haybati jalālihī kullu muʿānid, wa aṭfaʾa l-Lāhu bi-sirri nūrihī nāra kulli ʿaduwwin wa ḥāsid, alladhī jāʾa naʿtuhū fī kutubi s-sābiqīn, wa ʿammat barakatuhu l-awwalīna wa-l-ākhirīn, al-ghaythi l-midrār, alladhī haṭalat nafāʾisu durrihī ʿalā arḍī l-qulūb, fahtazzat wa-rabat wa-ṭmaʾannat li-rabbihā, fa-raʾati l-ḥaqqa ẓāhiran fa-ttabaʿat-h, wa-l-bāṭila rijsan fa-hajarat-h, ʿayni l-ʿulūmi l-ladunniyya, wa ghayni l-ghayrati l-intihāki l-ḥurumāti l-ilāhiyya, wa ʿalā ālihī wa sallim, wa adim barakātika ʿalayh, wa ʿalā ahli baytihi l-ladhīna adh-habta ʿanhumu r-rijsa wa ṭahhartahum taṭhīra.

O Allāh exalt our master Muḥammad, before whose awe-inspiring majesty every stubborn rejector submitted, and by the secret of whose light Allāh extinguished the fire of every enemy and envier. Whose descriptions came in the scriptures of the previous religious communities, and whose blessings covered both the earlier and later communities. The abundant rain whose precious pearls rained down upon the earths of the hearts, making them shake, grow, and find peace in their Lord, so that they saw the Truth apparent and followed it, and saw that falsehood was impure and abandoned it. The *ʿayn* of *ʿulūm* (knowledge) that comes from Allāh, and the *ghayn* of *ghayra* (zeal) for safeguarding what is sacred to Allāh. And exalt his folk and send greetings of peace. And keep Your blessings upon him constant, and upon the People of his Household from whom You removed all impurity and whom You purified most thoroughly.

اللّٰهُمَّ صَلِّ عَلَى سَيِّدِنَا مُحَمَّدْ ۞ الْبَرَكَةِ الْمُرْسَلَةِ مِنْ اللهِ ۞
وَالرَّحْمَةِ الْعَامَّةْ ۞ نَبِيِّ الرَّاحَةْ ۞ وَمَعْدِنِ الْفَصَاحَةْ ۞
صَاحِبِ الأَصْحَابْ ۞ نَبِيِّ التَّرْحَابْ ۞ نِعْمَ النَّبِيُّ الْقُرَشِيُّ
الْأَوَّابْ ۞ صَاحِبِ جِبْرِيلْ ۞ وَدَعْوَةِ الْخَلِيلْ ۞ ذِي
الرَّأْيِ السَّدِيدْ ۞ وَالْقَوْلِ الْمُفِيدْ ۞ وَالْأَمْرِ الْمَسْمُوعْ ۞
كَثِيرِ السَّهَرِ وَالْجُوعْ ۞ وَالْبُكَاءِ مِنْ خَشْيَةِ اللهِ بِالدُّمُوعْ
۞ الَّذِي كَانَ يَبْكِي لِجَلَالِكْ ۞ وَيَضْحَكُ لِجَمَالِكْ ۞
ذَلِكَ النَّبِيُّ الْعَالِي الْقَدْرْ ۞ صَاحِبُ أَهْلِ أُحُدٍ وَبَدْرْ ۞
فَاءُ فَلَاحِ الْمُؤْمِنِينْ ۞ وَقَافُ قُوتِ قُلُوبِ الْقَانِتِينْ ۞
وَعَلَى آلِهِ وَسَلِّمْ

Allāhumma ṣalli ʿalā sayyidinā Muḥammad, al-barakati l-mursalati min-Allāh, wa-r-raḥmati l-ʿāmma, nabiyyi r-rāḥa, wa maʿdini l-faṣāḥa, ṣāḥibi l-aṣḥāb, nabiyyi t-tarḥāb, niʿma n-nabiyyu l-qurashiyyu l-awwāb, ṣāḥibi Jibrīl, wa daʿwati l-Khalīl, dhi r-raʾyi s-sadīd, wa-l-qawli l-mufīd, wa-l-amri l-masmūʿ, kathīri s-sahari wa-l-jūʿ, wa-l-bukāʾi min khashyati l-Lāhi bi-d-dumūʿ, alladhī kāna yabkī li-jalālik, wa yaḍḥaku li-jamālik, dhālika n-nabiyyu l-ʿāli l-qadr, ṣāḥibu ahli Uḥud-in wa Badr, fāʾu falāḥi l-muʾminīn, wa qāfu qūti qulūbi l-qānitīn, wa ʿalā ālihī wa sallim.

O Allāh exalt our master Muḥammad. The blessing that was sent from Allāh, and the all-encompassing mercy. The Prophet of comfort, and the source of eloquence. Who was accompanied by the blessed Companions. The Prophet of welcoming others. The great Prophet from Quraysh. Of constant return to Allāh. The companion of Gabriel, and the supplication of Abraham the Intimate Friend of Allāh. Whose opinions are most correct, whose teachings are most beneficial, and whose commands are to be obeyed. Who stayed up late at night often in worship, and went hungry often. And cried tears from the fear of Allāh often. Who cried out of Your Majesty, and laughed out of Your Beauty. That Prophet of high worth. The companion of those who participated in Badr and Uhud. The *fāʾ* of the *falāḥ* (success) of the believers, and the *qāf* of the *qūt* (nourishment) of the hearts of the reverent. And exalt his folk and send greetings of peace.

اللّٰهُمَّ صَلِّ عَلَى سَيِّدِنَا مُحَمَّدٍ كَاشِفِ الْكُرَبِ لِلْمُتَوَسِّلِينْ
❁ وَعَظِيمِ الصِّلَةِ لِلْمُصَلِّينَ عَلَيْهِ وَالْمُسَلِّمِينْ ❁ السَّامِعِ
لِصَلَاتِهِمْ سَمَاعَ الْقَبُولْ ❁ وَالرَّادِّ لِسَلَامِهِمْ فَيَا نِعْمَ
الرَّسُولْ ❁ حَبِيبِ الْقُلُوبِ الْعَامِرَةْ ❁ وَجَلِيسِ الْأَعْيُنِ
السَّاهِرَةْ ❁ وَرُوحِ الْأَرْوَاحِ الطَّاهِرَةْ ❁ وَعِمَارَةِ الْأَفْئِدَةِ
الْعَامِرَةْ ❁ كَافِ الْكِفَايَةِ لِمَنْ اِحْتَمَى بِحِمَاهْ ❁ وَلَامِ اللَّذَّةِ
الْمُفَاضَةِ عَلَى أَوْلِيَاءِ اللهِ ❁ وَعَلَى آلِهِ وَسَلِّمْ

Allāhumma ṣalli ʿalā sayyidinā Muḥammad-in kāshifi l-kurabi li-l-mutawassilīn, wa ʿaẓīmi ṣ-ṣilati li-l-muṣallina ʿalayhi wa-l-musallimīn, as-sāmiʿi li-ṣalātihim samāʿa l-qabūl, wa-r-rāddi li-salāmihim fa-yā niʿma r-rasūl, ḥabībi l-qulūbi l-ʿāmira, wa jalīsi l-aʿyuni s-sāhira, wa rūḥi l-arwāḥi ṭ-ṭāhira, wa ʿimārati l-afʾidati l-ʿāmira, kāfi l-kifāyati li-man iḥtamā bi-ḥimāh, wa lāmi l-ladh-dhati l-mufāḍati ʿalā awliyāʾi l-Lāh, wa ʿalā ālihī wa sallim.

O Allāh exalt our master Muḥammad, the remover of distress for those who seek him as a means. Who creates a great connection with those who ask Allāh to exalt him and send him greetings of peace. Who hears their invocations with acceptance, and returns their greetings of peace, oh what a great Prophet! The beloved of light-filled hearts, and the sitting-companion of eyes that stay up at night. The life of pure souls, and the light that fills hearts that are alive. The *kāf* of *kifāya* (protection) for those who seek refuge in his safe quarter, and the *lām* of *ladh-dha* (pleasure) experienced by the Friends of Allāh. And exalt his folk and send greetings of peace.

اللّٰهُمَّ صَلِّ عَلَى سَيِّدِنَا مُحَمَّدٍ النَّبِيِّ الْمَقْبُولْ ۞ الْوَاصِلِ
الْمَوْصُولْ ۞ الْأَدْنَى إِلَيْكَ مِنْ كُلِّ دَانْ ۞ وَالْأَقْرَبِ
إِلَيْكَ مِنْ كُلِّ مَلَكٍ وَإِنْسَانْ ۞ عَيْنِ عِنَايَتِكَ السَّارِيَةِ
فِي الْخَلِيقَةْ ۞ الْجَامِعِ بَيْنَ عِلْمَيِّ الشَّرِيعَةِ وَالْحَقِيقَةْ ۞
صَاحِبِ الْفَتْحِ الَّذِي جَلَّ مِقْدَارُهْ ۞ وَالْإِمْدَادَاتِ الَّتِي
نَالَهَا زُوَّارُهْ ۞ الَّذِي جَلَى بِنُورِهِ السَّاطِعِ غَيَاهِبَ الظُّلُمَاتِ
وَالشُّرُورْ ۞ وَدَارَتْ بِبَرَكَةِ مَحَبَّتِهِ عَلَى أَهْلِ طَاعَتِهِ كُؤُوسُ
الْفَرَحِ وَالسُّرُورْ ۞ الَّذِي أَنْزَلْتَ عَلَيْهِ: ﴿ن وَالْقَلَمِ وَمَا
يَسْطُرُونْ﴾ ۞ وَأَنْزَلْتَ عَلَيْهِ: ﴿فَبِذٰلِكَ فَلْيَفْرَحُوا هُوَ
خَيْرٌ مِمَّا يَجْمَعُونْ﴾ ۞ مِيمِ الْمَجْدِ الدَّائِمْ ۞ وَنُونِ النُّورِ
السَّارِي فِي جَمِيعِ الْعَوَالِمْ ۞ وَعَلَى آلِهِ وَسَلِّمْ ۞ وَنَسْأَلُكَ
اللّٰهُمَّ شُهُودَ أَهْلِ الشُّهُودْ ۞ وَوُدَّ أَهْلِ الْوُدِّ يَا وَدُودْ

Allāhumma ṣalli ʿalā sayyidinā Muḥammad-in an-nabiyyi l-maqbūl, al-wāṣili l-mawṣūl, al-adnā ilayka min kulli dān, wa-l-aqrabi ilayka min kulli malakin wa insān, ʿayni ʿināyatika s-sāriyati fī l-khalīqa, al-jāmiʿi bayna ʿilmayyi sh-sharīʿati wa-l-ḥaqīqa, ṣāḥibi l-fatḥi l-ladhī jalla miqdāruh, wa-l-imdādāti l-lattī nālahā zuwwāruh, alladhī jalā bi-nūrihi s-sāṭiʿi ghayāhiba ẓ-ẓulumāti wa-sh-shurūr, wa dārat bi-barakati maḥabbatihī ʿalā ahli ṭāʿatihī kuʾūsu l-faraḥi wa-s-surūr, alladhī anzalta ʿalayh, ﴿nūn wa-l-qalami wa mā yasṭurūn﴾, wa anzalta ʿalayh, ﴿fa-bidhālika fa-l-yafraḥū huwa khayrun mimmā yajmaʿūn﴾, mīmi l-majdi d-dāʾim, wa nūni n-nūri s-sārī fī jamīʿi l-ʿawālim, wa

ʿalā ālihī wa sallim, wa nasʾaluka l-Lāhumma shuhūda ahli sh-shuhūd, wa wudda ahli l-wuddi yā Wadūd.

O Allāh exalt our master Muḥammad, the Prophet of Divine Acceptance, the Prophet of connection to You and arrival, who is closer to You than anyone who is close, and more proximate to You than any human or angel. The essence of Your Care which runs through all creation. Who combines the knowledge of both the Law and the Essential Reality. Whose spiritual illumination was truly great, and whose visitors receive his spiritual support. Who removed, by his shining light, the deep darknesses and evils. Whose cups of joy and happiness are given out to those who obey him, by the blessing of their love of him and his love of them. Upon whom You sent down, ﴿*Nūn, by the Pen and what they write.*﴾ and upon whom You sent down ﴿*In the grace and mercy of Allāh, in that let them rejoice, it is better than what they gather!*﴾ The *mīm* of eternal *majd* (glory), and the *nūn* of the *nūr* (light) that runs through all the worlds. And exalt his folk and send greetings of peace. And we ask You O Allāh for the spiritual witnessing of the people of spiritual witnessing, and the love of the people of love, O Loving One!

SALAT NUMBER SEVENTEEN

اللّٰهُمَّ صَلِّ عَلَى سَيِّدِنَا مُحَمَّدٍ فَخْرِ الْعَرَبْ ۞ النَّبِيِّ الْمُنْتَخَبْ
۞ أَفْضَلِ مَنْ عَرَجَ وَأَفْصَحِ مَنْ خَطَبْ ۞ الَّذِي أَزَلْتَ
بِهِ الْعَطَبْ ۞ وَفَرَّجْتَ بِهِ الْكُرَبْ ۞ نَبِيِّ الْوُدِّ لِلْوَدُودْ ۞
شَرِيفِ الْآبَاءِ وَالْجُدُودْ ۞ صَاحِبِ الدَّرَجَةِ الْعَالِيَةِ وَالْمَقَامِ
الْمَحْمُودْ ۞ نَبِيِّكَ الْمَحْمُودْ ۞ الَّذِي حَمِدَ النَّاسُ سِيرَتَهْ ۞
وَتَعَطَّرَ الْوُجُودُ بِذِكْرِهِ وَأَدَامَ اللهُ رِفْعَتَهْ ۞ قَائِدِ أُسْدِ الْوَغَى
۞ لِجِهَادِ مَنْ ضَلَّ وَطَغَى ۞ هَاءِ الْهِدَايَةِ وَ وَاوِ الْوِلَايَةْ ۞
وَعَلَى آلِهِ وَأَزْوَاجِهِ وَذُرِّيَّتِهِ وَأَهْلِ بَيْتِهْ ۞ وَسَلِّمْ تَسْلِيماً نَسْلَمُ
بِهِ مِنَ الْمَكَائِدْ ۞ وَنُكْفَى بِهِ شَرَّ كُلِّ بَاغٍ وَحَاسِدْ ۞ يَا
مُحِيطاً بِكُلِّ شَيْءْ ۞ وَيَا قَاهِراً فَوْقَ كُلِّ شَيْءْ ۞ وَيَا مَنْ
لَيْسَ كَمِثْلِهِ شَيْءٌ وَهُوَ السَّمِيعُ الْبَصِيرْ

Allāhumma ṣalli ʿalā sayyidinā Muḥammad-in fakhri l-ʿarab, an-nabiyyi l-muntakhab, afḍali man ʿaraja wa afṣaḥi man khaṭab, alladhī azalta bihi l-ʿaṭab, wa farrajta bihi l-kurab, nabiyyi l-wuddi li-l-Wadūd, sharīfi l-ābāʾi wa-l-judūd, ṣāḥibi d-darajati l-ʿāliyati wa-l-maqāmi l-maḥmūd, nabiyyika l-maḥmūd, alladhī ḥamida n-nāsu sīratah, wa taʿaṭṭara l-wujūdu bi-dhikrihī wa adāma l-Lāhu rifʿatah, qāʾidi usdi l-waghā, li-jihādi man ḍalla wa ṭaghā, hāʾi l-hidāyati wa wāwi l-wilāya, wa ʿalā ālihī wa azwājihī wa dhurriyyatihī wa ahli baytih, wa sallim taslīman naslamu bihī mina l-makāʾid, wa nukfā bihī sharra kulli bāghin wa ḥāsid, yā muḥīṭan bi-kulli shayʾ, wa yā qāhiran fawqa kulli shayʾ, wa yā man laysa ka-mithlihī shayʾun wa-huwa s-Samīʿ-u l-Baṣīr.

O Allāh exalt our master Muḥammad, the pride of the Arabs, the Chosen Prophet, the best to ascend above the heavens. The most eloquent of those who ever spoke. Through whom you removed different types of damage, and brought relief from different types of distress. The Prophet of love toward the Loving One. Of noble ancestors and forefathers. The one given the High Rank and the Praised Station. Your most-praised prophet, whose beautiful example was praised by the people. By whose mention all existence is perfumed, and who is constantly raised and elevated by Allāh. Commander of the lions of the battle field in the fight against the misguided oppressors. The *hā'* of *hidāya* (guidance), and the *wāw* of *wilāya* (proximity to Allāh). And exalt his folk, his wives, his progeny, and the People of his Household. And send greetings of peace in abundance, by the blessing of which we are secure from machinations, and protected from the evil of every transgressor and envier. O You who encompasses all things, O You who is the Subduer, above all else, O you who has no likeness and who is the all-Hearing the all-Seeing.

اللّٰهُمَّ صَلِّ عَلَى سَيِّدِنَا مُحَمَّدٍ ذِي الْوَقَارْ ۞ فَهُوَ خَيْرُ أُولِي
الْعَزْمِ وَالْهَيْبَةْ ۞ نَبِيِّ الرَّهْبَةِ وَالرَّغْبَةْ ۞ نَبِيِّ الْفَلاحْ ۞
الَّذِي خَضَعَتْ لِعِزَّتِهِ مُلُوكُ الْأَعَاجِمْ ۞ مُبِيدِ قَيْصَرَ وَكِسْرَى
وَكُلِّ ظَالِمْ ۞ الَّذِي بِهِ اللّٰهُ لَيْلاً أَسْرَى ۞ الَّذِي ارْتَقَى فَوْقَ
مَقَامِ الْخَلِيلْ ۞ وَدَنَا إِلَى مَكَانٍ تَأَخَّرَ عِنْدَهُ جِبْرِيلْ ۞ رَاءِ
الرَّحْمَةِ وَزَايِ الزَّكَاةْ ۞ وَعلَى آلِهِ وَصَحْبِهِ وَسَلِّمْ

Allāhumma ṣalli ʿalā sayyidinā Muḥammad-in dhi l-waqār, fa-huwa khayru uli l-ʿazmi wa-l-hayba, nabiyyi r-rahbati wa-r-raghba, nabiyyi l-falaḥ, alladhī khaḍaʿat li-ʿizzatihī mulūku l-aʿājim, mubīdi qayṣara wa kisrā wa kulli ẓālim, alladhī bihi l-Lāhu laylan asrā, alladhi r-taqā fawqa maqāmi l-Khalīl, wa danā ilā makānin taʾakh-khara ʿindahū Jibrīl, rāʾi r-raḥmati wa zāyi z-zakāt, wa ʿalā ālihī wa ṣaḥbihī wa sallim.

O Allāh exalt our master Muḥammad the dignified, for he is the best of those who show great resolve and inspire awe. The Prophet of fear and hope. The Prophet of success, to whose honour the foreign kings submitted. Who ended the rule of Ceasar, Chosroes and every oppressor. Whom Allāh took on a night journey, and who then ascended above the station of Abraham the Intimate Friend, and drew near to a place that Gabriel could not enter. The *rāʾ* of *raḥma* (mercy) and the *zāy* of *zakāt* (purifying charity). And upon his folk and Companions, and send greetings of peace.

اللّٰهُمَّ صَلِّ عَلَى سَيِّدِنَا مُحَمَّدٍ النَّبِيِّ الْأُمِّيِّ ۞ الَّذِي مِنْ عِلْمِهِ عِلْمُ اللَّوْحِ وَالْقَلَمْ ۞ وَمِنْ نُورِهِ ضَاءَ الْبَقِيعُ وَالْحَرَمْ ۞ الْمُخْبِرِ بِالْغَيْبِ عَنْ رَبِّ النَّاسْ ۞ وَالْمَعْنِيِّ بِالدِّفَاعِ عَنْهُ بِقَوْلِ رَبِّي: ﴿أَمْ يَحْسُدُونَ النَّاسْ﴾ ۞ سِينِ السَّعَادَةِ الْأَبَدِيَّةْ ۞ وَشِينِ الشُّكْرِ لِرَبِّ الْبَرِيَّةْ ۞ وَعَلَى آلِهِ وَأَصْحَابِهِ وَأَهْلِ بَيْتِهِ وَسَلِّمْ

Allāhumma ṣalli ʿalā sayyidinā Muḥammad-in an-nabiyyi l-ummī, alladhī min ʿilmihī ʿilmu l-lawḥi wa-l-qalam, wa min nūrihī ḍāʾa l-Baqīʿ-u wa-l-Ḥaram, al-mukhbiri bi-l-ghaybi ʿan Rabb-i n-Nās, wa-l-maʿniyyi bi-d-difāʿi ʿanhu bi-qawli rabbī, ﴿am yaḥsudūna n-nās﴾, sīni s-saʿādati l-abadiyya, wa shīni sh-shukri li-Rabb-i l-Bariyya, wa ʿalā ālihī wa aṣḥābihī wa ahli baytihī wa sallim.

O Allāh exalt our master Muḥammad the unlettered prophet, from whose knowledge comes the knowledge of the Tablet and the Pen, and by whose light the Sacred Sanctuary and the Baqīʾ Garden were illuminated. Who gave news from the unseen on behalf of the Lord of Creation. The one defended by Allāh's statement, ﴿*Or do they envy people?*﴾ (4:54) The *sīn* of eternal *saʿāda* (bliss) and the *shīn* of *shukr* (thankfulness) to the Lord of Creation. And exalt his folk, Companions, People of his Household, and send greetings of peace.

اللّٰهُمَّ صَلِّ عَلَى سَيِّدِنَا مُحَمَّدْ ❁ الْحَبِيبِ الَّذِي سَطَعَتْ
أَنْوَارُهْ ❁ وَسَارَتْ فِي الْأَكْوَانِ بِالْخَيْرِ أَخْبَارُهْ ❁ إِمَامِ
الْمُرْسَلِينَ الْأَمَاجِدْ ❁ وَكَلِيمِ الْأَحَدِ الْوَاحِدْ ❁ الَّذِي جَاءَ
حَقُّهُ فَدَمَغَ كُلَّ بَاطِلْ ❁ وَظَهَرَ عِلْمُهُ فَزَكَى كُلُّ عَامِلْ ❁
ذِي الْجَيْشِ الْغَالِبْ ❁ الَّذِي بِهِ تُنَالُ الرَّغَائِبْ ❁ وَعَلَى
أَصْحَابِهِ وَأَنْصَارِهِ وَأَزْوَاجِهِ وَذُرِّيَّتِهِ وَسَلِّمْ

Allāhumma ṣalli ʿalā sayyidinā Muḥammad, al-ḥabībi l-ladhī saṭaʿat anwāruh, wa sārat fi l-akwāni bi-l-khayri akhbāruh, imāmi l-mursalīna l-amājid, wa kalīmi l-Aḥad-i l-Wāḥid, alladhī jāʾa ḥaqquhū fa-damagha kulla bāṭil, wa ẓahara ʿilmuhū fa-zakā kullu ʿāmil, dhi l-jayshi l-ghālib, alladhī bihī tunālu r-raghāʾib, wa ʿalā aṣḥābihī wa anṣārihī wa azwājihī wa dhurriyyatihī wa sallim.

O Allāh exalt our master Muḥammad, the beloved whose lights shone, and whose news and teachings were carried across the worlds. The imam of the glorious messengers, and the one who spoke directly with the One and Unique. Whose truth came to obliterate every falsehood, and whose knowledge became well known, so that anyone who acts upon it is purified. Leader of the victorious army. Through whom cherished desires are obtained. And exalt his Companions, supporters, wives, and progeny, and send greetings of peace.

اللَّهُمَّ صَلِّ عَلَى سَيِّدِنَا مُحَمَّدٍ الْفَاتِحِ لِقُلُوبِ الْعَارِفِينَ بِنُورِ
سَنَاهْ ۞ وَالْبَاسِطِ بِالْمَعْرُوفِ يَدَهُ لِمَنْ نَحَا نَحْوَهُ يَوْمَ يَلْقَاهْ
۞ النَّبِيِّ الرَّاضِي الْمُرْتَضَى ۞ مَهْبِطِ الْوَحْيِ الْإِلٰهِيِّ وَمَنْبَعِ
الْفَضْلْ ۞ وَسِرِّ دَائِرَةِ الْعَدْلْ ۞ الْحَاكِمِ بِحُكْمِكَ مِنْ
فَوْقِ عَرْشِكْ ۞ وَالنَّاهِي بِنَهْيِكَ وَالْآمِرِ بِأَمْرِكْ ۞ الْهَاشِمِيِّ
ذِي السُّلَالَةِ الطَّاهِرَةِ النَّبَوِيَّةْ ۞ وَالذُّرِّيَّةِ الْبَاقِيَةِ الْمُبَارَكَةِ
التَّقِيَّةْ ۞ بَابِ اللهِ الْمَفْتُوحْ ۞ الرَّؤُوفِ الْحَلِيمِ الصَّفُوحْ
۞ ذِي الْأَمْنِ الْأَمِينْ ۞ مُحَمَّدٍ الْمَأْمُونْ ۞ مَوْضِعِ الْعِنَايَةِ
الرَّبَّانِيَّةْ ۞ ذِي الْأَسْرَارِ الْحَقِيقِيَّةْ ۞ وَالْعُلُومِ الْإِلٰهِيَّةْ ۞
وَالْقُوَّةِ الْهَاشِمِيَّةْ ۞ وَالرَّأْفَةِ الْمُحَمَّدِيَّةْ ۞ صَادِ الصِّدْقِ
وَضَادِ الضِّيَاءْ ۞ وَخَاتِمِ الْمُرْسَلِينَ وَالْأَنْبِيَاءْ ۞ صَلَاةً
تَنْحَلُّ بِهَا الْعُقَدْ ۞ مَصْحُوبَةً بِالْفَرَجْ ۞ عَلَى أَفْضَلِ مَنْ
أَسْرَى وَخَيْرِ مَنْ عَرَجْ ۞ وَعَلَى آلِهِ وَسَلِّمْ

Allāhumma ṣalli ʿalā sayyidinā Muḥammad-ini l-fātiḥi li-qulūbi l-ʿārifīna bi-nūri sanāh, wa-l-bāsiṭi bi-l-maʿrūfi yadahū li-man naḥā naḥwahū yawma yalqāh, an-nabiyyi r-rāḍī l-murtaḍā, mahbiṭi l-waḥyi l-ilāhiyyi wa manbaʿi l-faḍl, wa sirri dāʾirati l-ʿadl, al-ḥākimi bi-ḥukmika min fawqi ʿarshik, wa-n-nāhī bi-nahyika wa-l-āmiri bi-amrik, al-hāshimiyyi dhi s-sulālati ṭ-ṭāhirati n-nabawiyya, wa-dh-dhurriyyati l-bāqiyati l-mubārakati t-taqiyya, bābi l-Lāhi l-maftūḥ, ar-raʾūfi l-ḥalīmi ṣ-ṣafūḥ, dhi l-amni l-amīn, Muḥammad-ini l-maʾmūn, mawḍiʿi l-ʿināyati r-rabbāniyya, dhi l-asrāri l-ḥaqīqiyya, wa-

l-ʿulūmi l-ilāhiyya, wa-l-quwwati l-hāshimiyya, wa-r-raʾfati l-Muḥammad-iyya, ṣādi ṣ-ṣidqi wa ḍādi ḍ-ḍiyāʾ, wa khātimi l-mursalīna wa-l-anbiyāʾ, ṣalātan tanḥallu biha l-ʿuqad, maṣḥūbatan bi-l-faraj, ʿalā afḍali man asrā wa khayri man ʿaraj, wa ʿalā ālihī wa sallim.

O Allāh exalt our master Muḥammad who brings openings and illuminations to the hearts of the Knowers of Allāh through the flashing of his light. The one who will give a helping hand to those who come to him on the day they meet him. The Prophet who is pleased and well-pleasing. The receptacle of divine revelation and the well-spring of virtue. The centre of the sphere of justice. Who judged according to Your rulings which came from above Your throne. Who forbade according to Your prohibitions and commanded according to Your commandments. The Hashemite who is descended from a pure lineage of prophets. Fom whom came a never-ending line of blessed and pure descendants. The ever-open door of Allāh. The compassionate, the forbearing, the forgiving. The trustworthy and source of security. Muḥammad the entrusted. Who is surrounded by Lordly care. Possessor of secrets of essential realities and divine branches of knowledge. Who is characterised by Hashemite strength and Mohammedan compassion. The *ṣād* of *ṣidq* (truthfulness) and the *ḍāḍ* of *ḍiyāʾ* (illumination). The seal of the prophets and messengers. An exaltation through the blessings of which difficulties are removed and relief arrives. An exaltation of he who was the best to journey by night and the greatest to ascend the heavens. And exalt his folk and send greetings of peace.

اللّٰهُمَّ صَلِّ عَلَى سَيِّدِنَا مُحَمَّدْ ۞ كَعْبَةِ الْقَاصِدِينَ وَكَمَالِ كُلِّ
كَمَالْ ۞ الَّذِي جَاءَنَا بِالْإِخْلَاصِ فِي الْأَعْمَالْ ۞ الْآمِرِ
بِالثَّبَاتِ عِنْدَ الشَّدَائِدِ وَالْأَهْوَالْ ۞ الَّذِي وَعَدَ مَنْ صَبَرَ
بِالنَّصْرِ وَالنَّجَاةْ ۞ مَجْمَعِ الْجَمَالِ ذِي الْعِزِّ وَالْوِصَالْ ۞ صَلَاةً
تَحُولُ بِهَا بَيْنَنَا وَبَيْنَ الْجَوْرِ وَالْإِمْهَالْ ۞ وَعَلَى آلِهِ وَسَلِّمْ

Allāhumma ṣalli ʿalā sayyidinā Muḥammad, Kaʿbat-i l-qāṣidīna wa kamāli kulli kamāl, alladhī jāʾanā bi-l-ikhlāṣi fi l-aʿmāl, al-āmiri bi-th-thabāti ʿinda sh-shadāʾidi wa-l-ahwāl, alladhī waʿada man ṣabara bi-n-naṣri wa-n-najāt, majmaʿi l-jamāli dhi l-ʿizzi wa-l-wiṣāl, ṣalātan taḥūlu bihā baynanā wa bayna l-jawri wa-l-imhāl, wa ʿalā ālihī wa sallim.

O Allāh exalt our master Muḥammad the Kaʿba of the Seekers and the source of every perfection. Who came to teach us sincerity in actions. Who commanded us to stand firm in times of great difficulties and horrors. Who promised the patient ones victory and salvation. The convergence point of beauty. The honoured and connected one. An exaltation that comes between us and between any spiritual stalling or transgression. And exalt his folk and send greetings of peace.

SALAT NUMBER TWENTY-THREE

اللّٰهُمَّ صَلِّ عَلَى سَيِّدِنَا مُحَمَّدٍ الَّذِي شَرَحْتَ صَدْرَهُ بِقُدْرَتِكْ
۞ وَمَلَأْتَ قَلْبَهُ بِحِكْمَتِكْ ۞ وَقَلَّدْتَهُ سَيْفَ نَصْرِكْ
۞ وَرَفَعْتَ ذِكْرَهُ بِدَعْوَتِكْ ۞ وَأَقَمْتَهُ ظِلًّا ظَلِيلًا ۞
وَاتَّخَذْتَهُ حَبِيباً وَإِبْرَاهِيمَ خَلِيلًا ۞ طَاءِ الطَّهَارَةِ الْقَلْبِيَّةْ
۞ وَظَاءِ الظَّفَرِ عَلَى النُّفُوسِ الشَّيْطَانِيَّةْ ۞ وَعَلَى آلِهِ وَسَلِّمْ

Allāhumma ṣalli ʿalā sayyidinā Muḥammad-ini l-ladhī sharaḥta ṣadrahū bi-qudratik, wa malaʾta qalbahū bi-ḥikmatik, wa qalladtahū sayfa naṣrik, wa rafaʿta dhikrahū bi-daʿwatik, wa aqamtahū ẓillan ẓalīlā, wa-t-takhadhtahū ḥabīban wa Ibrāhīm-a khalīlā, ṭāʾi ṭ-ṭahārati l-qalbiyya, wa ẓāʾi ẓ-ẓafari ʿala n-nufūsi sh-shayṭāniyya, wa ʿalā ālihī wa sallim.

O Allāh exalt our master Muḥammad whose breast You expanded by Your might, and whose heart You filled with Your wisdom. Whom You garlanded with Your sword of victory, and whose mention You raised by Your call. Who You made a cooling shade (for others), and who You took as Your Beloved, while You took Abraham as Your Intimate Friend. The *ṭāʾ* of *ṭahāra* (purity) of the heart, and the *ẓāʾ* of *ẓafar* (victory) over satanic egos. And exalt his folk and send greetings of peace.

SALAT NUMBER TWENTY-FOUR

اللّٰهُمَّ صَلِّ عَلَى سَيِّدِنَا مُحَمَّدٍ صَلَاةَ الَّذِي يُصَلِّي عَلَيْهِ
تَعْظِيماً لِقَدْرِهْ ۞ وَبَارِكْ عَلَيْهِ بَرَكَةً تَعُودُ عَلَيْنَا بِجَمِيلِ
سِرِّهْ ۞ النَّبِيِّ الْوَفِيِّ خَيْرِ مَنْ وَافَى الْمَحْشَرْ ۞ وَأَفْضَلِ مَنْ
دَعَا إِلَيْكَ وَهَذَّبَ النُّفُوسَ وَذَكَّرْ ۞ وَعَلَى آلِهِ وَسَلِّمْ

Allāhumma ṣalli ʿalā sayyidinā Muḥammad-in ṣalāta l-ladhī yuṣallī ʿalayhi taʿẓīman li-qadrih, wa bārik ʿalayhi barakatan taʿūdu ʿalaynā bi-jamīli sirrih, an-nabiyyi l-wafiyyi khayri man wāfa l-maḥshar, wa afḍali man daʿā ilayka wa hadh-dhaba n-nufūsa wa dhakkar, wa ʿalā ālihī wa sallim.

O Allāh exalt our master Muḥammad, an exaltation like those that are requested by those who ask You to exalt him out of veneration of his worth. And bless him with a blessing that returns to us with a secret gift. The loyal prophet, the best of those who will come to the Plain of Resurrection. The best of those who invited others to You, disciplined the souls, and reminded them of You. And exalt his folk, and send greetings of peace.

اللّٰهُمَّ صَلِّ عَلَى ذِي الْعِصْمَةِ الرَّبَّانِيَّةِ وَالشِّرْعَةِ الْحَنِيفِيَّةْ ۞
سَيِّدِنَا مُحَمَّدٍ الْمُتَخَلِّقِ بِالْقُرْآنِ الْعَظِيمْ ۞ وَالَّذِي يُسْتَسْقَى
الْغَمَامُ بِوَجْهِهِ الْكَرِيمْ ۞ نَبِيِّ الْأُمَّةِ الْمَرْحُومَةِ بِبَعْثَتِهْ ۞
النَّزِيهِ الْوَجِيهِ الْمُجَابِ فِي دَعْوَتِهْ ۞ ذِي الْهَيْبَةِ وَالْأَسْرَارْ ۞
وَالسَّكِينَةِ وَالْوَقَارْ ۞ الْقَائِلِ لِصَاحِبِهِ إِذْ هُمَا فِي الْغَارْ ۞
﴿لَا تَحْزَنْ إِنَّ اللهَ مَعَنَا﴾ ۞ ﴿فَأَنْزَلَ اللهُ سَكِينَتَهُ عَلَيْهْ﴾
۞ صَاحِبِ السَّجْدَةِ فِي الْمَحْشَرْ ۞ حِينَمَا تُسْنَدُ الشَّفَاعَةُ
إِلَيْهْ ۞ الطَّيِّبِ الطَّبِيبْ ۞ ذِي الْقَلْبِ الْمُنِيبْ ۞ وَالرَّأْيِ
الْمُصِيبْ ۞ وَالْفَتْحِ الْقَرِيبْ ۞ الْمُسَمَّى عِنْدَ اللهِ بِالْحَبِيبْ
۞ الْمُجَابِ الْمُجِيبْ ۞ وَعَلَى آلِهِ وَأَدِمِ اللّٰهُمَّ سَلَامَكَ عَلَيْهِ
وَعَلَى أَهْلِ بَيْتِهْ ۞ وَأَصْحَابِهِ وَأَزْوَاجِهِ وَذُرِّيَّتِهِ أَجْمَعِينْ

Allāhumma ṣalli ʿalā dhi l-ʿiṣmati r-rabbāniyyati wa-sh-shirʿati l-ḥanīfiyya, sayyidinā Muḥammad-ini l-mutakhalliqi bi l-Qurʾān-i l-ʿaẓīm, wa-l-ladhī yustasqa l-ghamāmu bi-wajhihi l-karīm, nabiyyi l-ummati l-marḥūmati bi-baʿthatih, an-nazīhi l-wajīhi l-mujābi fī daʿwatih, dhi l-haybati wa-l-asrār, wa-s-sakīnati wa-l-waqār, al-qāʾili li-ṣāḥibihī idh humā fi l-ghār, ﴿lā taḥzan inna l-Lāha maʿanā﴾ ﴿fa anzala l-Lāhu sakīnatahū ʿalayh﴾, ṣāḥibi s-sajdati fi l-maḥshar, ḥīnamā tusnadu sh-shafāʿatu ilayh, aṭ-ṭayyibi ṭ-ṭabīb, dhi l-qalbi l-munīb, wa-r-raʾyi l-muṣīb, wa-l-fatḥi l-qarīb, al-musammā ʿinda l-Lāhī bi-l-Ḥabīb, al-mujābi l-mujīb, wa ʿalā ālihī wa-adimi l-Lāhumma salāmaka ʿalayhi wa ʿalā ahli baytih, wa aṣḥābihī wa azwājihī wa dhurriyyatihī ajmaʿīn.

O Allāh exalt the one who is under divine protection from sin and error, and who came with the primordial monotheistic Sharīʿah. Our master Muḥammad whose character is that of the Majestic Qurʾān. Through the rank of his noble face rain is asked for, and is sent down. The Prophet of the Ummah that was blessed with Divine Mercy through his sending. The eminent one, of greatest integrity, whose supplications are answered. The possessor of secrets. Who inspired awe in others, and was characterised by tranquility and dignity. Who said to his companion when they were in the cave, ﴿*Do not be sad, for Allāh is with us.*﴾ ﴿*Then Allāh brought down tranquility upon him*﴾ (9:40). The one who will prostrate on the Plain of Resurrection when the role of intercession is granted to him. The healer, the pure one. Whose heart was always turning to Allāh and attached to Him. Whose opinion was always correct. The cause of quick openings and illumination. Who is known with Allāh as "The Beloved." The one who responds to Allāh and to whose supplications Allāh responds. And exalt his folk, and send constant greetings of peace upon him, the People of his Household, his Companions, wives, and all his progeny.

اللّٰهُمَّ صَلِّ عَلَى سَيِّدِنَا مُحَمَّدْ ۞ الْفَاتِحِ لِأَقْفَالِ الْقُلُوبِ
بِمِفْتَاحِ حِكَمِ أَسْرَار ﴿وَعَلَّمَكَ مَا لَمْ تَكُنْ تَعْلَم﴾ ۞
الرَّؤُوفِ الرَّحِيمْ ۞ الَّذِي هُوَ بِالْمُؤْمِنِ مِنْ أَبِيهِ وَأُمِّهِ أَرْحَمْ
۞ الْآخِذِ بِحُجَزِ أُمَّتِهِ مِنَ الْوُقُوعِ فِي النَّارْ ۞ وَالْمُقَسِّمِ
لِنَعِيمِ الْجَنَّةِ بِإِذْنِ الْعَزِيزِ الْغَفَّارْ ۞ وَعَلَى آلِهِ وَسَلِّمْ

Allāhumma ṣalli ʿalā sayyidinā Muḥammad, al-fātiḥi li-aqfāli l-qulūbi bi-miftāḥi ḥikami asrār, ﴿wa ʿallamaka mā lam takun taʿlam﴾, ar-raʾūfi r-raḥīm, alladhī huwa bi-l-muʾmini min abīhi wa ummihī arḥam, al-ākhidhi bi-ḥujazi ummatihī mina l-wuqūʿi fi n-nār, wa-l-muqassimi li-naʿīmi l-jannati bi-idhni l-ʿAzīz-i l-Ghaffār, wa ʿalā ālihī wa sallim.

O Allāh exalt our master Muḥammad. The opener of the locks of the hearts by the key of the wisdom containing the secrets of ﴿*He taught you what you did not know*﴾ (4:113). The compassionate and merciful. Who is more merciful to the believer than his own father and mother. Who grabs the garments of the believers to save them from falling into the Fire. And who divides the bliss of Paradise upon its inhabitants by the permission of the Mighty, the Forgiving. And exalt his folk and send greetings of peace.

اللّٰهُمَّ صَلِّ عَلَى سَيِّدِنَا مُحَمَّدٍ النَّبِيِّ الْوَصِيِّ ۞ النَّبِيِّ الأُمِّيِّ ۞ النَّبِيِّ الصَّفِيِّ ۞ النَّبِيِّ الْعَرَبِيِّ ۞ الْخِيَارِ الْمُخْتَارْ ۞ زَائِدِ الْوَقَارِ كَثِيرِ الْأَنْوَارْ ۞ الشَّهِيدِ الْمُشَاهِدِ لِلْأَنْوَارِ الْمَلَكِيَّةْ ۞ الْعَابِدِ الْوَرِعِ الزَّاهِدْ ۞ السَّيِّدِ الْمُتَوَاضِعْ ۞ الْمُهَابِ الْخَاشِعْ ۞ خَيْرِ النَّاسْ ۞ وَأَنْفَعِ النَّاسِ لِلنَّاسْ ۞ مِفْتَاحِ كُلِّ خَيْرْ ۞ وَمِغْلَاقِ كُلِّ شَرّْ ۞ صَلَاةً تَكُونُ سَبَباً مُوَصِّلاً إِلَى مَرْضَاتِكْ ۞ وَعَلَى آلِهِ وَسَلِّمْ بِعَدَدِ أَنْفَاسِ مَخْلُوقَاتِكْ

Allāhumma ṣalli ʿalā sayyidinā Muḥammad-ini n-nabiyyi l-waṣī, an-nabiyyi l-ummī, an-nabiyyi ṣ-ṣafī, an-nabiyyi l-ʿarabī, al-khiyāri l-mukhtār, zāʾidi l-waqāri kathīri l-anwār, ash-shahīdi l-mushāhidi li-l-anwāri l-malakiyya, al-ʿābidi l-wariʿi z-zāhid, as-sayyidi l-mutawāḍiʿ, al-muhābi l-khāshiʿ, khayri n-nās, wa anfaʿi n-nāsi li-n-nās, miftāḥi kulli khayr, wa mighlāqi kulli sharr, ṣalātan takūnu sababan muwaṣṣilan ilā marḍātik, wa ʿalā ālihī wa sallim bi-ʿadadi anfāsi makhlūqatik.

O Allāh exalt our master Muḥammad the Prophet, the Divinely Appointed Trustee. The unlettered Prophet. The pure-hearted Prophet. The Arabian Prophet. The Chosen One, the Favoured One. The dignified one, the illumined one. The Witness who witnesses the angelic lights. The devout worshiper, the ascetic, the scrupulous. The humble master. The reverent one who inspires awe in others. The best of people, and the most beneficial of people to people. The key to every good, and the lock to every evil. An exaltation that brings Your pleasure for those who request it. And exalt his folk, and send greetings of peace as many times as the number of Your creations.

SALAT NUMBER TWENTY-EIGHT

اللّٰهُمَّ صَلِّ عَلَى سَيِّدِنَا مُحَمَّدٍ صَلَاةً مِنْ لَدُنْكَ إِلَيْهِ ۞ وَسَلِّمْ
وَبَارِكْ عَلَيْهِ ۞ بِعَدَدِ بَرَكَاتِكَ النَّازِلَةِ مِنْ سَمَائِكَ إِلَى
أَرْضِكَ ۞ وَالْخَارِجَةِ مِنْ أَرْضِكَ إِلَى خَلْقِكَ ۞ وَاجْزِهِ عَنَّا
اللّٰهُمَّ أَحْسَنَ الْجَزَاءِ ۞ وَارْزُقْنَا اللّٰهُمَّ بِفَضْلِكَ الصَّفَاءَ
وَالْوَفَاءَ ۞ يَا حَكِيمُ يَا عَلِيمْ

Allāhumma ṣalli ʿalā sayyidinā Muḥammad-in ṣalātan min ladunka ilayh, wa sallim wa bārik ʿalayh, bi-ʿadadi barakātika n-nāzilati min samāʾika ilā arḍik, wa-l-khārijati min arḍika ilā khalqik, wa-jzihī ʿannā l-Lāhumma aḥsana l-jazāʾ, wa-r-zuqna l-Lāhumma bi-faḍlika ṣ-ṣafāʾa wa-l-wafāʾ, yā Ḥakīm-u yā ʿAlīm.

O Allāh exalt our master Muḥammad, an exaltation that comes from Your presence to him. And send blessings and greetings of peace. As many times as the number of Your blessings which descend from Your sky to Your earth. And the blessings which come out of Your earth to Your creations. And reward him, O Allāh, on our behalf the most excellent reward. And grant us purity and loyalty by Your grace O Allāh, O Most Wise, O Most Knowledgeable.

اللّٰهُمَّ صَلِّ عَلَى سَيِّدِنَا مُحَمَّدٍ جَدِّ الْحَسَنَيْنْ ۞ وَخَيْرِ الْفَرِيقَيْنْ ۞ وَإِمَامِ الْقِبْلَتَيْنْ ۞ وَقُرَّةِ كُلِّ عَيْنْ ۞ سِرَاجِ الدَّارَيْنْ ۞﴿وَثَانِيَ اثْنَيْنْ﴾۞ الْمُنَزَّهِ عَنْ كُلِّ شَيْنْ ۞ وَالْمُزِيلِ بِنُورِهِ كُلَّ غَيْنْ ۞ ذِي الْفَضَائِلِ الْعَمِيمَةْ ۞ وَالطَّرِيقَةِ الْمُسْتَقِيمَةْ ۞ الْهَاشِمِيِّ الشَّرِيفْ ۞ وَالْقُرَشِيِّ الْعَفِيفْ ۞ صَلاةً تَشْرَحُ بِهَا صَدْرِي ۞ وَتَضَعُ بِهَا وِزْرِي ۞ وَتُيَسِّرُ بِهَا أَمْرِي ۞ وَتَرْفَعُ بِهَا ذِكْرِي ۞ وَتُدِيمُ بِهَا أَجْرِي ۞ وَتُبَارِكُ بِهَا فِي عُمْرِي ۞ وَعَلَى آلِهِ وَأَصْحَابِهْ ۞ وَأَهْلِ بَيْتِهِ وَأَزْوَاجِهْ ۞ وَذُرِّيَّتِهِ أَجْمَعِينْ

Allāhumma ṣalli ʿalā sayyidinā Muḥammad-in jaddi l-ḥasanayn, wa khayri l-farīqayn, wa imāmi l-qiblatayn, wa qurrati kulli ʿayn, sirāji d-dārayn, ﴾wa thāni-athnayn,﴿ al-munazzahi ʿan kulli shayn, wa-l-muzīli bi-nūrihī kulla ghayn, dhi l-faḍāʾili l-ʿamīma, wa-ṭ-ṭarīqati l-mustaqīma, al-hāshimiyyi sh-sharīf, wa-l-qurashiyyi l-ʿafīf, ṣalātan tashraḥu bihā ṣadrī, wa taḍaʿu bihā wizrī, wa tuyassiru bihā amrī, wa tarfaʿu bihā dhikrī, wa tudīmu bihā ajrī, wa tubāriku bihā fī ʿumrī, wa ʿalā ālihī wa aṣḥābih, wa ahli baytihī wa azwājih, wa dhurriyyatihī ajmaʿīn.

O Allāh exalt our master Muḥammad the grandfather of al-Ḥasan and al-Ḥusayn. The best of the two groups (mankind and jinn) and the imam of the two Qiblas. The joy of every eye. The sun of both abodes (this world and the next). ﴾*One of only two*﴿ (9:40) (in the Cave when Allāh was their third). Who is free of every fault, and who removes, through his light, every dark cloud. Whose virtues are all-encompassing, and whose path is the straight path. The noble Hashemite and immaculate Qurayshi. An exaltation through the blessing of which You expand my breast, remove my burdens, put ease in my affairs, raise my mention, prolong my rewards, and bless my lifespan. And exalt his folk, Companions, People of his Household, wives, and all his progeny.

SALAT NUMBER THIRTY

اللّٰهُمَّ صَلِّ عَلَى سَيِّدِنَا مُحَمَّدْ ۞ بَحْرُ الْعُلُومِ الْمُتَلَاطِمَةِ أَمْوَاجُهَا ۞ وَقَمَرُ الْأُمَّةِ الْمُنِيرُ سِرَاجُهَا ۞ الَّذِي بِهِ تُزَالُ الْكُرَبُ فَهُوَ فَرَّاجُهَا ۞ وَالَّذِي أُنْزِلَتْ عَلَيْهِ شِرْعَةُ الأُمَّةِ وَمِنْهَاجُهَا ۞ سَيْفُ اللهِ الْمَسْلُولْ ۞ وَنَبِيُّ الرَّحْمَةِ الْمَرْسُولْ ۞ الْوَجِيهُ الْمَقْبُولْ ۞ وَعَلَى آلِهِ وَأَصْحَابِهْ ۞ وَأَهْلِ بَيْتِهِ وَأَحْبَابِهْ ۞ وَعَلَى الْمُؤْمِنِينَ وَالْمُؤْمِنَاتْ ۞ وَالْمُسْلِمِينَ وَالْمُسْلِمَاتْ ۞ وَسَلِّمْ تَسْلِيماً كَثِيرَا

Allāhumma ṣalli ʿalā sayyidinā Muḥammad, baḥru l-ʿulūmi l-mutalāṭimati amwājuhā, wa qamaru l-ummati l-munīru sirājuhā, alladhī bihī tuzālu l-kurabu fa-huwa farrājuhā, walladhī unzilat ʿalayhi shirʿatu l-ummati wa minhājuhā, sayfu l-Lāh-i l-maslūl, wa nabiyyu r-raḥmati l-marsūl, al-wajīhu l-maqbūl, wa ʿalā ālihī wa aṣḥābih, wa ahli baytihī wa aḥbābih, wa ʿala l-muʾminīna wa-l-muʾmināt, wa-l-muslimīna wa-l-muslimāt, wa sallim taslīman kathīra.

O Allāh exalt our master Muḥammad. The ocean of sciences whose waves crash against each other. The illuminating full moon of this Ummah and its sun. Through whom distressful matters are removed for he is the bringer of relief. Upon whom was revealed the Sharīʿah of the Ummah and its way. The unsheathed sword of Allāh. The Prophet who was sent as a mercy. The eminent and accepted in the sight of Allāh. And exalt his folk, his Companions, the People of his Household, and his beloveds. And exalt the believing men and believing women, and Muslim men and Muslim women. And send greetings of peace in abundance.

اللّٰهُمَّ صَلِّ عَلَى سَيِّدِنَا مُحَمَّدٍ الْحَامِدِ الْمَحْمُودْ ۞ وَالْفَاقِدِ
لِلْمَفْقُودْ ۞ وَالْمُشَاهِدِ لِلْمَوْجُودْ ۞ أَفْضَلِ عَابِدٍ لِلْمَلِكِ
الْمَعْبُودْ ۞ وَخَيْرِ مُتَقَرِّبٍ لِلّٰهِ بِالسُّجُودْ ۞ أَوْفَى النَّاسِ
بِالْعُهُودْ ۞ الَّذِي لَمْ يَخْرُجْ عَنْ حَضْرَةِ الشُّهُودْ ۞ الْمُمْتَلِئِ
الْقَلْبِ مِنْ وُدِّ الْوَدُودْ ۞ الْحَاكِمِ بِالشَّرْعِ وَالْمُقِيمِ
لِلْحُدُودْ ۞ أَفْضَلَ صَلَاةٍ وَأَزْكَى سَلَامْ ۞ بِعَدَدِ كُلِّ مَعْلُومٍ
وَمَعْدُودْ ۞ وَعَلَى إِخْوَانِهِ مِنَ الْأَنْبِيَاءِ وَالْمُرْسَلِينْ ۞ وَعَلَى
أَهْلِ بَيْتِهِ الْمُطَهَّرِينْ ۞ وَأَزْوَاجِهِ وَذُرِّيَّتِهِ الْمُبَارَكِينْ ۞
وَنَسْأَلُكَ اللّٰهُمَّ خَيْرَ الدُّنْيَا وَالْآخِرَةْ ۞ وَالْفُتُوحَ وَالنَّصْرْ
۞ يَا مَنْ بِيَدِهِ الْأَمْرْ ۞﴿أَلَا إِلَى اللهِ تَصِيرُ الْأُمُورْ﴾

Allāhumma ṣalli ʿalā sayyidinā Muḥammad-ini l-ḥāmidi l-maḥmūd, wa-l-fāqidi li-l-mafqūd, wa-l-mushāhidi li-l-mawjūd, afḍali ʿābidin li-l-Malik-i l-maʿbūd, wa khayri mutaqarribin li-l-Lāh-i bi-s-sujūd, awfa n-nāsi bi-l-ʿuhūd, alladhī lam yakhruj ʿan ḥaḍrati sh-shuhūd, al-mumtaliʾi l-qalbi min wuddi l-Wadūd, al-ḥākimi bi-sh-sharʿi wa-l-muqīmi li-l-ḥudūd, afḍala ṣalātin wa azkā salām, bi-ʿadadi kulli maʿlūmin wa maʿdūd, wa ʿalā ikhwānihī mina l-anbiyāʾi wa-l-mursalīn, wa ʿalā ahli baytihi l-muṭahharīn, wa azwājihī wa dhurriyyatihi l-mubārakīn, wa nasʾaluka l-Lāhumma khayra d-dunyā wa-l-ākhira, wa-l-futūḥa wa-n-naṣr, yā man bi-yadihi l-amr, ﴿alā ila l-Lāh-i taṣīru l-umūr﴾

O Allāh exalt our master Muḥammad. The praised one, the one who praises You. The one who does not see non-being, and witnesses the Real Being. The best worshiper of the King, the Worshiped One. And the best who draws near to Allāh through prostration. The most faithful of people in fulfilling oaths. Who never left the presence of divine witnessing. Whose heart was filled with love of the Loving One. Who judged by the Sharīʿah and upheld its prescribed punishments. The best exaltation and the purest greeting of peace. As many times as the number of all things in Your Knowledge. And exalt his brothers the other prophets and messengers. And exalt the purified People of his Household, his blessed wives, and his progeny. And we ask You O Allāh for the good of this world and the next, and openings and victory. O you in whose Hand is the affair.

﴾*To Allāh all things return*﴿ (42:53).

SALAT NUMBER THIRTY-TWO

اللّٰهُمَّ صَلِّ عَلَى سَيِّدِنَا مُحَمَّدٍ صَلَاةَ الْفَرَجِ الْقَرِيبْ ۞
وَعَلَى آلِهِ وَسَلِّمْ بِعَدَدِ كُلِّ سِرٍّ عَجِيبْ

Allāhumma ṣalli ʿalā sayyidinā Muḥammad-in ṣalāta l-faraji l-qarīb, wa ʿalā ālihī wa sallim bi-ʿadadi kulli sirrin ʿajīb.

O Allāh exalt our master Muḥammad, an exaltation through the blessing of which quick relief arrives. And exalt his folk and send greetings of peace, as many times as the number of every wondrous secret.

SALAT NUMBER THIRTY-THREE

اللّٰهُمَّ صَلِّ عَلَى سَيِّدِنَا مُحَمَّدْ ۞ النَّبِيِّ الْبَدْرِ الْمُنِيرْ ۞
وَرَحْمَةِ اللَّطِيفِ الْخَبِيرْ ۞ وَعَلَى آلِهِ وَسَلِّمْ

Allāhumma ṣalli ʿalā sayyidinā Muḥammad, an-nabiyyi l-badri l-munīr, wa raḥmati l-Laṭīfi l-Khabīr, wa ʿalā ālihī wa sallim.

O Allāh exalt our master Muḥammad, the Prophet, the luminous full moon. The mercy of the Most Subtle, the Most Aware. And exalt his folk and send greetings of peace.

SALAT NUMBER THIRTY-FOUR

اللّٰهُمَّ صَلِّ عَلَى سَيِّدِنَا مُحَمَّدْ ✿ الْأَوَّلِ وَالْخَاتِمْ ✿ نَبِيِّ
الْمَرَاحِمْ ✿ وَعَلَى آلِهِ وَسَلِّمْ

Allāhumma ṣalli ʿalā sayyidinā Muḥammad, al-awwali wa-l-khātim, nabiyyi l-marāḥim, wa ʿalā ālihī wa sallim.

O Allāh exalt our master Muḥammad, the first and the seal, the prophet of vast mercies, and exalt his folk and send greetings of peace.

SALAT NUMBER THIRTY-FIVE

اللّٰهُمَّ صَلِّ عَلَى سَيِّدِنَا مُحَمَّدْ ✿ صَلَاةَ جَمِيعِ الْمَخْلُوقَاتِ
عَلَيْهْ ✿ وَسَلِّمْ عَلَيْهِ سَلامَهُمْ ✿ وَأَدِمْ ذٰلِكَ إِلَى مَا شَاءَ اللهْ
✿ وَعَلَى آلِهِ فِي كُلِّ لَمْحَةٍ وَنَفَسٍ عَدَدَ مَا وَسِعَهُ عِلْمُ اللهِ

Allāhumma ṣalli ʿalā sayyidinā Muḥammad, ṣalāta jamīʿi l-makhlūqāti ʿalayh, wa sallim ʿalayhi salāmahum, wa adim dhālika ilā mā shāʾ Allāh, wa ʿalā ālihī fī kulli lamḥatin wa nafasin ʿadada mā wasiʿahū ʿilmu l-Lāh.

O Allāh exalt our master Muḥammad, with the exaltations requested for him by all creatures, and send him their greetings of peace, and let that continue until what Allāh wills. And exalt his folk, with every glance and every breath, as many times as all that is encompassed by the knowledge of Allāh.

SALAT NUMBER THIRTY-SIX

اللّٰهُمَّ صَلِّ أَفْضَلَ صَلَاةٍ عَلَى أَفْضَلِ رَسُولْ ۞ سَيِّدِنَا مُحَمَّدٍ النَّبِيِّ الْمَأْمُولْ ۞ وَارْزُقْنِي اللّٰهُمَّ السَّخَاءَ وَالْقَبُولْ ۞ وَعَلَى آلِهِ وَسَلِّمْ

Allāhumma ṣalli afḍala ṣalātin ʿalā afḍali rasūl, sayyidinā Muḥammad-in an-nabiyyi l-maʾmūl, wa-r-zuqni l-Lāhumma s-sakhāʾa wa-l-qabūl, wa ʿalā ālihī wa sallim.

O Allāh exalt the greatest messenger with the greatest exaltation. Our master Muḥammad the Prophet in whom we place our hopes. And grant me O Allāh Your generosity and acceptance. And exalt his folk and send greetings of peace.

SALAT NUMBER THIRTY-SEVEN

اللّٰهُمَّ صَلِّ عَلَى سَيِّدِنَا مُحَمَّدْ ۞ نَبِيِّ الْحَمْدْ ۞ وَمَعْدِنِ الْمَجْدْ ۞ أَفْضَلِ مَنْ جَاهَدَ وَجَدّْ ۞ وَعَلَى آلِهِ وَسَلِّمْ

Allāhumma ṣalli ʿalā sayyidinā Muḥammad, nabiyyi l-ḥamd, wa maʿdini l-majd, afḍali man jāhada wa jadd, wa ʿalā ālihī wa sallim

O Allāh exalt our master Muḥammad, the prophet of praise, the source of glory, the greatest of those who strived with seriousness. And exalt his folk and send greetings of peace.

SALAT NUMBER THIRTY-EIGHT

اللَّهُمَّ صَلِّ عَلَى سَيِّدِنَا مُحَمَّدٍ نَبِيِّ الْكَرَامَةْ ۞ وَصَاحِبِ
الزَّعَامَةْ ۞ الشَّفِيعِ يَوْمَ الْقِيَامَةْ ۞ وَعَلَى آلِهِ وَسَلِّمْ

Allāhumma ṣalli ʿalā sayyidinā Muḥammad-in nabiyyi l-karāma, wa ṣāḥibi z-zaʿāma, ash-shafīʿi yawma l-qiyāma, wa ʿalā ālihī wa sallim

O Allāh exalt our master Muḥammad the Prophet of Honour, the leader, the intercessor on the Day of Resurrection. And exalt his folk and send greetings of peace.

SALAT NUMBER THIRTY-NINE

اللَّهُمَّ صَلِّ عَلَى سَيِّدِنَا مُحَمَّدْ ۞ الْحَافِظِ بِنُورِ جَلَالِهِ
صَحِيحَ مَقَالِهْ ۞ وَعَلَى آلِهِ وَسَلِّمْ

Allāhumma ṣalli ʿalā sayyidinā Muḥammad, al-ḥāfiẓi bi-nūri jalālihī ṣaḥīḥa maqālih, wa ʿalā ālihī wa sallim.

O Allāh exalt our master Muḥammad, whose lights of majesty ensured the preservation of his authentic sayings, and exalt his folk and send greetings of peace.

SALAT NUMBER FORTY

اللّٰهُمَّ صَلِّ عَلَى سَيِّدِنَا مُحَمَّدٍ خَيْرِ الْأَنَامْ ۞ وَمِصْبَاحِ الظَّلَامْ ۞ وَرَسُولِ اللهِ الْمَلِكِ الْعَلَّامْ ۞ الْمُصَلِّي بِاللَّيْلِ وَالنَّاسُ نِيَامْ ۞ وَارْزُقْنَا حُسْنَ الْخِتَامْ

Allāhumma ṣalli ʿalā sayyidinā Muḥammad-in khayri l-anām, wa miṣbāḥi ẓ-ẓalām, wa rasūli l-Lāh-i l-Malik-i l-ʿallām, al-muṣallī bi-l-layli wa-n-nāsu niyām, wa-r-zuqnā ḥusna l-khitām.

O Allāh exalt our master Muḥammad the best of people. The lamp in the darkness. The Messenger of the King, the Most Knowledgeable. Who prayed at night while people slept. And grant us a good and excellent end to our lives.

سُبْحَانَ اللهِ عَدَدَ خَلْقِهِ ۞ سُبْحَانَ اللهِ زِنَةَ عَرْشِهِ ۞
سُبْحَانَ اللهِ رِضَاءَ نَفْسِهِ ۞ سُبْحَانَ اللهِ مِدَادَ كَلِمَاتِهِ
﴿سُبْحَانَ رَبِّكَ رَبِّ الْعِزَّةِ عَمَّا يَصِفُونَ ۞ وَسَلَامٌ عَلَى
الْمُرْسَلِينَ ۞ وَالْحَمْدُ لِلَّهِ رَبِّ الْعَالَمِينَ﴾

SubḥānAllāh-i ʿadada khalqih, subḥānAllāh-i zinata ʿarshih, subḥānAllāh-i riḍāʾa nafsih, subḥānAllāh-i midāda kalimātih, ﴾subḥāna rabbika rabbi l-ʿizzati ʿammā yaṣifūn, wa salāmun ʿala l-mursalīn, wa-l-ḥamdu li-l-Lāhi Rabbi l-ʿĀlamīn﴿.

'Glory be to Allāh' to the number of His creations. 'Glory be to Allāh' to the weight of His Throne. 'Glory be to Allāh' as much as His pleasure. 'Glory be to Allāh' as much as the ink of His words. ﴾*Glory be to Your Lord, the Lord of Might, above what they describe, and peace be upon the messengers, and all praise is due to Allāh, Lord of the Worlds*﴿ (37:180-2).

الصَّلَوَاتُ الثَّلَاثُون لِجَعْلِ مَا قُدِّرَ يَهُون

Thirty Ṣalawāt for Easing that which has been Decreed

by Shaykh ʿAbd al-Ghanī al-Jaʿfarī

اَللّٰهُمَّ صَلِّ عَلَى سَيِّدِنَا مُحَمَّدٍ صَلَاةً تُنَوِّرُ بِهَا وُجُوهَنَا

Allāhumma ṣalli ʿalā sayyidinā Muḥammad-in ṣalātan tunawwiru bihā wujūhanā

O Allāh exalt our master Muhammad, an exaltation through which You illuminate our faces

اَللّٰهُمَّ صَلِّ عَلَى سَيِّدِنَا مُحَمَّدٍ صَلَاةً تَشْرَحُ بِهَا صُدُورَنَا

Allāhumma ṣalli ʿalā sayyidinā Muḥammad-in ṣalātan tashraḥu bihā ṣudūranā

O Allāh exalt our master Muhammad, an exaltation through which You expand our breasts with light

اَللّٰهُمَّ صَلِّ عَلَى سَيِّدِنَا مُحَمَّدٍ صَلَاةً تُطَهِّرُ بِهَا قُلُوبَنَا

Allāhumma ṣalli ʿalā sayyidinā Muḥammad-in ṣalātan tuṭahhiru bihā qulūbanā

O Allāh exalt our master Muhammad, an exaltation through which You cleanse our hearts

اَللّٰهُمَّ صَلِّ عَلَى سَيِّدِنَا مُحَمَّدٍ صَلَاةً تُرَوِّحُ بِهَا أَرْوَاحَنَا

Allāhumma ṣalli ʿalā sayyidinā Muḥammad-in ṣalātan turawwiḥu bihā arwāḥanā

O Allāh exalt our master Muhammad, an exaltation through which You refresh our spirits

اَللّٰهُمَّ صَلِّ عَلَى سَيِّدِنَا مُحَمَّدٍ صَلَاةً تُزَكِّي بِهَا نُفُوسَنَا

Allāhumma ṣalli ʿalā sayyidinā Muḥammad-in ṣalātan tuzakkī bihā nufūsanā

O Allāh exalt our master Muhammad, an exaltation through which You purify our souls

اَللّٰهُمَّ صَلِّ عَلَى سَيِّدِنَا مُحَمَّدٍ صَلَاةً تَغْفِرُ بِهَا ذُنُوبَنَا

Allāhumma ṣalli ʿalā sayyidinā Muḥammad-in ṣalātan taghfiru bihā dhunūbanā

O Allāh exalt our master Muhammad, an exaltation through which You forgive our sins

اَللّٰهُمَّ صَلِّ عَلَى سَيِّدِنَا مُحَمَّدٍ صَلَاةً تَسْتُرُ بِهَا عُيُوبَنَا

Allāhumma ṣalli ʿalā sayyidinā Muḥammad-in ṣalātan tasturu bihā ʿuyūbanā

O Allāh exalt our master Muhammad, an exaltation through which You hide our faults

اَللّٰهُمَّ صَلِّ عَلَى سَيِّدِنَا مُحَمَّدٍ صَلَاةً تَضَعُ بِهَا أَوْزَارَنَا

Allāhumma ṣalli ʿalā sayyidinā Muḥammad-in ṣalātan taḍaʿu bihā awzāranā

O Allāh exalt our master Muhammad, an exaltation through which You remove our burdens

اَللّٰهُمَّ صَلِّ عَلَى سَيِّدِنَا مُحَمَّدٍ صَلَاةً تُثَقِّلُ بِهَا مِيزَانَنَا

Allāhumma ṣalli ʿalā sayyidinā Muḥammad-in ṣalātan tuthaqqilu bihā mīzānanā

O Allāh exalt our master Muhammad, an exaltation through which You add weight to our scales

اَللّٰهُمَّ صَلِّ عَلَى سَيِّدِنَا مُحَمَّدٍ صَلَاةً تَقْضِي بِهَا حَاجَاتِنَا

Allāhumma ṣalli ʿalā sayyidinā Muḥammad-in ṣalātan taqḍī bihā ḥājātinā

O Allāh exalt our master Muhammad, an exaltation through which You fulfil our needs

اَللّٰهُمَّ صَلِّ عَلَى سَيِّدِنَا مُحَمَّدٍ صَلَاةً تَشْفِي بِهَا مَرِيضَنَا

Allāhumma ṣalli ʿalā sayyidinā Muḥammad-in ṣalātan tashfī bihā marīḍanā

O Allāh exalt our master Muhammad, an exaltation through which You heal our sick

اَللّٰهُمَّ صَلِّ عَلَى سَيِّدِنَا مُحَمَّدٍ صَلَاةً تُسْعِدُ بِهَا شَقِيَّنَا

Allāhumma ṣalli ʿalā sayyidinā Muḥammad-in ṣalātan tusʿidu bihā shaqiyyanā

O Allāh exalt our master Muhammad, an exaltation through which You make our wretched people of felicity

اَللّٰهُمَّ صَلِّ عَلَى سَيِّدِنَا مُحَمَّدٍ صَلَاةً تُوَسِّعُ بِهَا أَرزَاقَنَا

Allāhumma ṣalli ʿalā sayyidinā Muḥammad-in ṣalātan tuwassiʿu bihā arzāqanā

O Allāh exalt our master Muhammad, an exaltation through which You expand our sustenance

اَللّٰهُمَّ صَلِّ عَلَى سَيِّدِنَا مُحَمَّدٍ صَلَاةً تُيَسِّرُ بِهَا أُمُورَنَا

Allāhumma ṣalli ʿalā sayyidinā Muḥammad-in ṣalātan tuyassiru bihā umūranā

O Allāh exalt our master Muhammad, an exaltation through which You put ease in our affairs

اَللّٰهُمَّ صَلِّ عَلَى سَيِّدِنَا مُحَمَّدٍ صَلَاةً تَرْفَعُ بِهَا ذِكْرَنَا

Allāhumma ṣalli ʿalā sayyidinā Muḥammad-in ṣalātan tarfaʿu bihā dhikranā

O Allāh exalt our master Muhammad, an exaltation through which You exalt our mention

اَللّٰهُمَّ صَلِّ عَلَى سَيِّدِنَا مُحَمَّدٍ صَلَاةً تُؤَيِّدُ بِهَا أَمْرَنَا

Allāhumma ṣalli ʿalā sayyidinā Muḥammad-in ṣalātan tuʾayyidu bihā amranā

O Allāh exalt our master Muhammad, an exaltation through which You support us in our affairs

اَللّٰهُمَّ صَلِّ عَلَى سَيِّدِنَا مُحَمَّدٍ صَلَاةً تُعَظِّمُ بِهَا أَجْرَنَا

Allāhumma ṣalli ʿalā sayyidinā Muḥammad-in ṣalātan tuʿaẓẓimu bihā ajranā

O Allāh exalt our master Muhammad, an exaltation through which You increase our reward

اَللّٰهُمَّ صَلِّ عَلَى سَيِّدِنَا مُحَمَّدٍ صَلَاةً تَمُدُّ بِهَا أَعْمَارَنَا

Allāhumma ṣalli ʿalā sayyidinā Muḥammad-in ṣalātan tamuddu bihā aʿmāranā

O Allāh exalt our master Muhammad, an exaltation through which You increase our lifespans

اَللّٰهُمَّ صَلِّ عَلَى سَيِّدِنَا مُحَمَّدٍ صَلَاةً تَقْبَلُ بِهَا أَعْمَالَنَا

Allāhumma ṣalli ʿalā sayyidinā Muḥammad-in ṣalātan taqbalu bihā aʿmālanā

O Allāh exalt our master Muhammad, an exaltation through which You accept our actions

اَللّٰهُمَّ صَلِّ عَلَى سَيِّدِنَا مُحَمَّدٍ صَلَاةً تَحْفَظُ بِهَا أَسْرَارَنَا

Allāhumma ṣalli ʿalā sayyidinā Muḥammad-in ṣalātan taḥfaẓu bihā asrāranā

O Allāh exalt our master Muhammad, an exaltation through which You guard our secrets

اَللّٰهُمَّ صَلِّ عَلَى سَيِّدِنَا مُحَمَّدٍ صَلَاةً تُنَزِّهُ بِهَا أَفْكَارَنَا

Allāhumma ṣalli ʿalā sayyidinā Muḥammad-in ṣalātan tunazzihu bihā afkāranā

O Allāh exalt our master Muhammad, an exaltation through which You elevate our thoughts

اَللّٰهُمَّ صَلِّ عَلَى سَيِّدِنَا مُحَمَّدٍ صَلَاةً تُصَفِّي بِهَا أَكْدَارَنَا

Allāhumma ṣalli ʿalā sayyidinā Muḥammad-in ṣalātan tuṣaffī bihā akdāranā

O Allāh exalt our master Muhammad, an exaltation through which You cleanse our impurities

اَللّٰهُمَّ صَلِّ عَلَى سَيِّدِنَا مُحَمَّدٍ صَلَاةً تُنَوِّرُ بِهَا أَبْصَارَنَا

Allāhumma ṣalli ʿalā sayyidinā Muḥammad-in ṣalātan tunawwiru bihā abṣāranā

O Allāh exalt our master Muhammad, an exaltation through which You illuminate our sight

اَللّٰهُمَّ صَلِّ عَلَى سَيِّدِنَا مُحَمَّدٍ صَلَاةً تَفْتَحُ بِهَا بَصَائِرَنَا

Allāhumma ṣalli ʿalā sayyidinā Muḥammad-in ṣalātan taftaḥu bihā baṣāʾiranā

O Allāh exalt our master Muhammad, an exaltation through which You open our inner sight

اَللّٰهُمَّ صَلِّ عَلَى سَيِّدِنَا مُحَمَّدٍ صَلَاةً تُقَوِّي بِهَا عَزَائِمَنَا

Allāhumma ṣalli ʿalā sayyidinā Muḥammad-in ṣalātan tuqawwī bihā ʿazāʾimanā

O Allāh exalt our master Muhammad, an exaltation through which You strengthen our determination

اَللّٰهُمَّ صَلِّ عَلَى سَيِّدِنَا مُحَمَّدٍ صَلَاةً تُهَوِّنُ بِهَا مَصَائِبَنَا

Allāhumma ṣalli ʿalā sayyidinā Muḥammad-in ṣalātan tuhawwinu bihā maṣāʾibanā

O Allāh exalt our master Muhammad, an exaltation through which You ease our calamities

اَللّٰهُمَّ صَلِّ عَلَى سَيِّدِنَا مُحَمَّدٍ صَلَاةً نَجْتَازُ بِهَا صِرَاطَنَا

Allāhumma ṣalli ʿalā sayyidinā Muḥammad-in ṣalātan najtāzu bihā ṣirāṭanā

O Allāh exalt our master Muhammad, an exaltation with which we traverse our path

اَللّٰهُمَّ صَلِّ عَلَى سَيِّدِنَا مُحَمَّدٍ صَلَاةً تَهْزِمُ بِهَا عَدُوَّنَا

Allāhumma ṣalli ʿalā sayyidinā Muḥammad-in ṣalātan tahzimu bihā ʿaduwwanā

O Allāh exalt our master Muhammad, an exaltation through which You vanquish our enemies

اَللّٰهُمَّ صَلِّ عَلَى سَيِّدِنَا مُحَمَّدٍ صَلَاةً تَخْتِمُ بِهَا حَيَاتَنَا

Allāhumma ṣalli ʿalā sayyidinā Muḥammad-in ṣalātan takhtimu bihā ḥayātanā

O Allāh exalt our master Muhammad, an exaltation because of which You seal our lives with a good end

اَللّٰهُمَّ صَلِّ عَلَى سَيِّدِنَا مُحَمَّدٍ صَلَاةً تُطَيِّبُ بِهَا قُبُوْرَنَا

Allāhumma ṣalli ʿalā sayyidinā Muḥammad-in ṣalātan tuṭayyibu bihā qubūranā

O Allāh exalt our master Muhammad, an exaltation through which You fragrance our graves

فَاتِحَةُ الأَقْفَال

The Opener of Locks

بِسْمِ ٱللَّهِ ٱلرَّحْمَٰنِ ٱلرَّحِيمِ

يَا رَبِّ عَجِّلْ بِالْهُدَى لِلْفَانِيْ
Make haste, my Lord, to guide this short-lived slave,

قَبْلَ حُلُوْلِ الْجِسْمِ فِي الأَكْفَانِ
Before my body's shrouded, in its grave;

وَرُدَّهُ نَحْوَ الْهُدَى بِالْحِكْمَةِ
And drive this body back to guidance wise,

حَتَّى يَكُوْنَ قَائِماً بِالشِّرْعَةِ
That by Your Sacred Law it lives and dies;

يَا رَبِّ وَاقْبَلْ دَعْوَتِي فَإِنِّي
My plea accept, my Lord! Myself I scold,

عَبْدٌ مُلِيمٌ مُحْسِنٌ بِالظَّنِّ

Of You the highest thought I firmly hold;

فَلَا تُخَيِّبْ سَيِّدِي رَجَائِي

My hopes do not let down, my Lord! Agree

إِقْبَلْ إِلٰهِي كَرَماً دُعَائِي

To grant what I request, through Charity!

وَحُفَّنِي بِلُطْفِكَ الْعَظِيمِ

Surround me in Your Kindness, that's immense;

وَعُمَّنِي بِفَضْلِكَ الْعَمِيمِ

Include me in Your vast Benevolence!

تِجَارَتِي هِيَ الذُّنُوبُ حَقّاً

As trade, I give You nothing save my vice:

وَلَمْ أَكُن بِدَعْوَتِي مُحِقّاً

My claims are hollow, though they may sound nice;

وَقَدْ دَعَانِي لِلْهَوَى شَيْطَانِي

My Satan prompted me to heed my whims,

وَفِي عَظِيمِ الذَّنْبِ قَدْ رَمَانِي

He threw me into dangerous, great sins;

وَأَنْتَ رَبُّ الْجُودِ وَالْجَلَالِ

You're Lord of Majesty, and You're most kind,

وَتَغْفِرُ الذَّنْبَ وَلَا تُبَالِي

Forgiving any sin You do not mind;

وَمَا سِوَاكَ أَحَدٌ أَدْعُوهُ

There's none, apart from You, to hear my pleas:

يَسِّرْ إِلٰهِي كُلَّ مَا أَرْجُوهُ

In all that I request, Lord, grant me ease!

بِمَا دَعَاكَ آدَمٌ وَنُوحُ

By Adam's pleas, and Noah's, made to You,

وَكُلُّ عَبْدٍ فِي الدُّجَى يَنُوحُ

And every cry of slaves, at night, to You,

وَدَعْوَةِ الْخَلِيلِ إِبْرَاهِيمِ

And prayers, made to You, by Abraham,

وَدَعْوَةِ الذَّبِيحِ وَالْكَلِيمِ

By Moses, and the one saved by Your ram,

بِمَا دَعَاكَ يُونُسُ بْنُ مَتَّى

And he who cried to You, inside the whale

فِي ظُلْمَةِ اللَّيْلِ وَقَدْ أَجَبْتَ

In darkness, and was saved from his travail,

وَزَكَرِيَّاءُ الَّذِي نَاجَاكَ

And Zachariah whispering to You

بِدَعْوَةٍ خَفِيَّةٍ دَعَاكَ

With secret prayers, calling out to You,

إِنِّي بِمَا دَعَوْكَ يَا مُجِيبُ

By these I'll not be failed, You Who Reply,

أَدْعُوكَ فِي الْخَفَاءِ لَا أَخِيبُ

When I, in turn, to You, in secret cry!

بِمَا دَعَا يَعْقُوبُ فِي اللَّيَالِي

By that which every night, Jacob requested,

وَكُمَّلُ النِّسَاءِ وَالرِّجَالِ

By pleas from men and women You've perfected,

بِمَا دَعَاكَ يُوسُفٌ فِي الْجُبِّ

By Joseph's cry to You, inside the well,

إِكْشِفْ إِلٰهِي مَا بِنَا مِنْ كَرْبِ

Remove, my God, the hardship that befell!

أَدْعُوكَ رَبِّي دَعْوَةَ الْكَئِيبِ

I pray to You, my Lord, as one forlorn,

اَلْحَائِرِ الْمِسْكِينِ وَالْغَرِيبِ

Confused, in dire need, from all withdrawn,

وَدَعْوَةَ الْمَظْلُومِ وَالْمَكْرُوبِ

The call of one oppressed, by mishaps harmed,

يَا دَافِعاً لِلْهَمِّ وَالْكُرُوبِ

O You Who Clears unease, and all alarms!

بِمَا دَعَا عِيسَى مِنَ الدُّعَاءِ

By what You heard from Jesus, in his pleas,

وَمَا لَهُ فِي النَّاسِ مِنْ شِفَاءِ

Through which he cured the sick from all disease,

بِمَا دَعَا نَبِيُّكَ الْمَقْبُولُ

The prayers of Your Prophet, the accepted,

مُحَمَّدٌ شَفِيعُنَا الرَّسُولُ

Our Intercessor sent, by You selected,

وَرَحْمَةُ اللهِ إِلَى الْعِبَادِ

The Mercy of Allāh to all He made,

يَسِّرْ لَنَا يَارَبِّ بِالرَّشَادِ

Through guidance help us find Your ease and shade!

إِفْتَحْ لَنَا مَا سُدَّ مِنْ أَقْفَالِ

Make open for us locks that have been closed,

وَعُمَّنَا بِالْخَيْرِ وَالنَّوَالِ

Ensure that by Your Goodness we're enclosed!

يَا عَالِمٌ وَخَالِقٌ مُرِيدُ

O Knower and Creator, Who Desires,

يَسِّرْ لَنَا يَارَبِّ مَا نُرِيدُ

Make easy for us, Lord, what we desire!

فَكُلُّ خَيْرٍ مِنْكَ نَرْتَجِيهِ

So every goodness that, of You, we ask:

يَسِّرْ لَنَا الْخَيْرَ وَبَارِكْ فِيهِ

Allow us, in it, ease and blessings vast!

وَاكْتُبْ لَنَا بِفَضْلِكَ السَّلَامَةَ

And by Your Grace, decree that there's no threat

مِنْ كُلِّ مَا يُفْضِي إِلَى النَّدَامَةْ

To us of doing that which we regret!

وَامْنَعْ دَوَاعِي الشَّرِّ مِنْ حِمَانَا

Drive those that call to evil from our space!

وَرُدَّهُمْ فِي نَحْرِهِمْ عِدَانَا

The harm that others mean us, let them face!

وَكِدْ لِأَعْدَائِي جَمِيعاً كَيْدَا

Against my foes make mighty plots! If these

وَمَنْ يُرِيدُ السُّوءَ قَدْ تَرَدَّى

Should wish me harm, allow that they be seized

فِي حُفْرَةِ السُّوءِ الَّذِي نَوَاهُ

By all the harm that they, for me, prepare,

وَمَا نَوَاهُ مِنْ أَذَى يَلْقَاهُ

And let them be entrapped in their own snare!

يَا نَاصِرَ الْمَظْلُومِ وَالْمَقْهُورِ

O Helper of Your wronged, downtrodden slaves,

يَا بَاعِثَ الْمَوْتَى مِنَ الْقُبُورِ

O Raiser of the dead, up from their graves,

إِبْعَثْ عَلَيْهِمْ فِتْنَةً وَطَرْدَا

Raise up for them tough trials and expel

سُحْقاً لَهُمْ عَنْ حَيِّنَا وَبُعْدَا

Them far from where we are and crush them well!

يَا حَيُّ يَا قَيُّومُ يَا جَبَّارُ

O Living O Sustainer, Who Renews!

مُنْتَقِمٌ وَغَالِبٌ قَهَّارُ

Avenger, Dominator, Who Subdues!

وَيَا شَدِيدَ الْبَطْشِ يَا قَوِيُّ

Whose strike is most severe, Immensely Strong

وَيَا عَظِيمَ الْقَهْرِ يَا عَلِيُّ

With Power to Subdue, On High Enthroned!

عَجِّلْ لِأَحْبَابِي بِكُلِّ خَيْرِ

Make haste for those I love, with good from You,

وَكُلِّ مَرْغُوبٍ بِكُلِّ يُسْرِ

And ease in all they want – a gift from You!

وَكُنْ لَهُمْ يَا سَيِّدِي مُعِيناً

My Master, be for them a source of aid,

ومُنْجِياً وحَافِظاً أَمِينَا

A Saviour, Guarding all, safe in Your shade!

وَالْأَهْلِ وَالْأَنْجَالِ وَالْإِخْوَانِ

My children and my brothers, all my folk:

وَرُدَّ عَنْهُمْ فِتْنَةَ الشَّيْطَانِ

Push back, away from them, the Devil's yoke!

ثُمَّ الصَّلَاةُ بِالسَّلَامِ السَّامِي

And then may peace and blessings rain upon,

عَلَى النَّبِيِّ نَاصِرِ الْإِسْلَامِ

A Prophet sent, Defender of Islam,

وَآلِهِ الْأَطْهَارِ آلِ الْمَرْحَمَةْ

His Family the pure, with mercy blessed,

وَصَحْبِهِ الْأَمْجَادِ أَهْلِ الْمَلْحَمَةْ

And his Companions brave, in battle dress!

وَالْجَعْفَرِيُّ صَالِحٌ يَكُونُ

Al-Ja'farī, named Ṣāliḥ: may he rest,

فِي جَنَّةِ الْخُلْدِ كَذَا مَصُونُ

Like them in Paradise, with safety blessed!

دَعْوَةُ الْيُسْرِ الْقَرِيبْ

بِإِذْنِ اللهِ السَّمِيْعِ الْمُجِيبْ

The Prayer for Swift Relief and Ease

By the Permission of Allāh,
the All-Hearing, the One Who Answers

بِسْمِ ٱللَّهِ ٱلرَّحْمَٰنِ ٱلرَّحِيمِ

حَمْداً لِمَوْلَانَا الْكَرِيمِ الْبَاقِي

We praise our Noble Lord, Who's always there,

مُيَسِّرِ الْأُمُورِ وَالْأَرْزَاقِ

Sustaining us, and easing our affairs;

ثُمَّ الصَّلَاةُ بِالسَّلَامِ النَّامِي

And then may peace and blessings rain upon

عَلَى النَّبِيِّ قُدْوَةِ الْأَنَامِ

A Prophet sent to be our paragon;

وآلِهِ الْأَفَاضِلِ الْأَطْهَارِ

And on his Folk, the bless'd and purified,

وَصَحْبِهِ الْأَمَاجِدِ الْأَخْيَارِ

And His Companions chosen, magnified!

يَا مَنْ إِلَيْهِ تُرْجَعُ الْأُمُورُ

O You by Whom all matters are reformed,

وَمَنْ هُوَ اللَّطِيفُ وَالْخَبِيرُ

And Who is Gently Kind and All-Informed;

وَمَنْ إِلَيْهِ تُرْفَعُ الْأَكُفُّ

O You to Whom our hands are humbly raised,

وَمَنْ لَهُ الصَّلَاةُ إِذْ نُصَفُّ

By worshipers in ranks You're daily praised;

وَمَنْ إِلَيْهِ تَسْجُدُ الْجِبَاهُ

And You before whom foreheads are prostrate:

وَمَا لَنَا مِنْ خَالِقٍ سِوَاهُ

Apart from You, no being can create;

وَمَنْ عَلَيْهِ قَصْدُنَا يَهُونُ

And You for whom our goals are nothing grand:

يَقُولُ كُنْ بِأَمْرِهِ يَكُونُ

Say 'Be!' and then it is, by Your command;

اِفْتَحْ لَنَا مَا سُدَّ مِنْ أَبْوَابِ

Unlock all doors for us, our gracious Lord,

بِالْخَيْرِ وَالْقَبُولِ وَالثَّوَابِ
With goodness and acceptance and reward!

سَخِّرْ لَنَا الْقُلُوبَ وَالْأَرْوَاحَا
Let hearts and souls attend to what we need,

هَيِّئْ لَنَا مِنْ أَمْرِنَا فَلَاحَا
Prepare for us success in all our deeds!

وَمَا لَنَا مُدَبِّرٌ سِوَاكَ
And no one governs things for us save You:

أَجِبْ عُبَيْداً سَيِّدِي دَعَاكَ
Respond! Your little slave cries out to You!

أَنْتَ الْكَرِيْمُ ذُو الْعَطَاءِ الدَّائِمْ
You're Generous, Your Giving never ends,

وَالْفَضْلِ وَالْإِحْسَانِ وَالْمَرَاحِمْ
Through Gracious Mercies, sent with Excellence,

يَا سَابِغٌ لِنِعَمٍ عَظِيمَة
O You from Whom descend our blessings vast,

ظَاهِرَةٍ بَاطِنَةٍ مُقِيمَة
Both outwardly and inwardly held fast,

كَنِعْمَةِ النَّبِيِّ وَالْقُرآنِ
Your blessings like the Prophet and Quran,

وَنِعْمَةِ الْإِسْلَامِ وَالْإِيمَانِ
And blessings like our faith, and our Islam;

يَا سَامِعٌ لِلْهَمْسِ فِي الظَّلَامِ

O You Who hears the whispers that we hide,

وَرَازِقَ الْخَفِيِّ فِي الْآكَامِ

Who secretly and outwardly provides,

وَرَازِقٌ بِلُطْفِهِ الْأَجِنَّة

Sustaining, gently, babies yet unborn,

فِي عَالَمِ الْأَرْحَامِ مُطْمَئِنَّة

At rest in wombs all day from eve till morn;

يَا رَازِقَ الْمَدْفُونِ فِي التُّرَابِ

Provider of those buried in the ground:

مِنْ غَيْرِ مَا كَسْبٍ وَلَا اكْتِسَابِ

They never earned Your gifts, which they just found;

وَكُلُّ مَرْزُوقٍ لَهُ أَرْزَاقُ

Whoever gets provisions, they're from You:

لَدَيْكَ يَا اللهُ يَا خَلَّاقُ

From You, Allāh, creating all that's new;

وَالْخَيْرُ مِنْكَ نَازِلٌ كَثِيرُ

And Good descends, so much that no one counts,

وَالْفَضْلُ مِنْكَ رَبَّنَا كَبِيرُ

And Grace from You, our Lord, in large amounts;

يَا وَاسِعَ الرَّحْمَةِ يَا رَحْمٰنُ

O You of Mercy vast, and with no bound,

حَنَّانُ يَا رَحِيمُ يَا مَنَّانُ
You're Tender, granting Mercy all around;

اِغْفِرْ ذُنُوبِي يَا إِلٰهِي غَفْرَا
Forgive my sins, my God, and spare not one,

وَاسْتُرْ عُيُوبِي يَا إِلٰهِي سَتْرَا
And hide my faults, my God, from everyone!

يَا غَافِرَ الذَّنْبِ أَيَا تَوَّابُ
Forgiver of all sins, O You Who Turns,

يَا رَاحِمَ الضَّعِيفِ يَا وَهَّابُ
O Giver: for the weak You show concern;

هَبْ لِي عُلُوماً رَبَّنَا وَحِكْمَة
Lord: sciences and wisdom grant to me,

وَحَجَّةً مَبْرُورَةً وَرَحْمَة
A Hajj that you accept, and clemency!

بِالْعَفْوِ جُدْ يَا رَبَّنَا وَالْعَافِيَة
With pardon and good health, our Lord, be free,

وَعِيشَةٍ نَقِيَّةٍ وَرَاضِيَة
And grant a life that's pure and leaves us pleased!

وَرُدَّ عَنَّا يَا إِلٰهَ النَّاسِ
Drive back from us, O God of all mankind,

أَهْلَ الْهَوَى والشَّرِّ وَالْوَسْوَاسِ
The ones with evil promptings in their minds!

وَحَسْبُنَا اللهُ وَنِعْمَ الْكَافِي

Allāh's enough for us, the best Defence

لِكُلِّ ظَاهِرٍ وَكُلِّ خَافِي

From those we see, and those we cannot sense. (x3)

نِعْمَ الْوَكِيلُ أَنْتَ يَا قَهَّارُ

The Best Protector, You are All-Compelling,

نِعْمَ الْحَسِيبُ أَنْتَ يَا جَبَّارُ

The Best to take Account, all foes Repelling.

فَوَّضْتُ أَمْرِي دَائِماً إِلَيْكَ

To You I leave, forever, all that's mine:

كَذَا اعْتِمَادِي خَالِقِي عَلَيْكَ

My Maker, I depend on Your Design.

فَلَا أُبَالِي إِنْ رَضِيتَ عَنِّي

If You are pleased with me, what do I care?

فَلِلسِّوَى وَالْغَيْرِ لَا تَكِلْنِي

So place me not in someone else's care!

يَا حَيُّ يَا قَيُّومُ يَا سَلَامُ

O Living, O Sustainer, Free of Blame,

يَا مَانِعُ امْنَعْ مَا بِهِ نُلَامُ

O Guardian, hold back what brings us shame!

وَحُفَّنَا بِلُطْفِكَ الْخَفِيِّ

Your Subtle Kindness! Drown us in its seas,

فِي كُلِّ مَا يَجْرِي مِنَ الْمَقْضِيِّ

With all that reaches us from Your Decrees! (x3)

بِلُطْفِكَ الْمُصْحِبِ لِلْأَقْدَارِ

By Kindness that's attached to what's foreknown,

أَكُونُ مَخْفِيّاً عَنِ الْأَشْرَارِ

To troublemakers let me be unknown!

بِلُطْفِكَ الظَّاهِرِ وَالْمَنْظُورِ

By Kindness in the open, unconstrained,

أَكُونُ مَحْفُوفاً لَدَى الْمَقْدُورِ

May I be sheltered in what You've ordained!

بِلُطْفِكَ الْكَافِيْ لِمَنْ دَعَاكَ

By Kindness that's enough for those who pray,

أَكُونُ يَا مَوْلَايَ فِي حِمَاكَ

In Your safekeeping, Master, let me stay!

بِلُطْفِكَ الْحَاصِلِ عِنْدَ الشِّدَّة

By Kindness which comes down in times severe,

أَنْزِلْ عَلَيْنَا الْحُبَّ وَالْمَوَدَّة

Send down upon us love, and tender care!

بِلُطْفِكَ الْحَاصِلِ لِلْأَمْوَاتِ

By Kindness which comes down for those who've died,

أَكُونُ مَلْحُوظاً لَدَى الْمَمَاتِ

Once I am gone, may thoughts of me abide!

بِلُطْفِكَ الْخَافِي عَنِ الْأَبْصَارِ
By Kindness that's obscured from people's sight,

أَكُونُ مَأْمُوناً مِنَ الْأَكْدَارِ
Allow me to be safe from every blight!

بِلُطْفِكَ النَّازِلِ عِنْدَ الْجَدْبِ
By Kindness coming down when there's no rain,

وَلُطْفِكَ الْحَاصِلِ عِنْدَ الْكَرْبِ
And in disasters filled with loss and pain,

وَلُطْفِكَ الْمُنْقِذِ لِلْمَسْجُوْنِ
And Kindness saving those that have been jailed,

وَلُطْفِكَ الْمُفْرِجِ لِلْمَحْزُوْنِ
And for the sad, it has their gloom regaled,

وَلُطْفِكَ الدَّائِمِ بِالْأَلْطَافِ
And Kindness that is always manifest,

أَنْزِلْ لَنَا مَوَائِدَ الْأَضْيَافِ
Bring down the banquets that You serve Your guests!

فَقَطْرَةٌ مِنْ لُطْفِهِ تَحْمِينَا
One drop of Kindness will provide our shield!

وَقَطْرَةٌ مِنْ جُوْدِهِ تَكْفِينَا
One drop of Giving quite enough will yield!

إِنْ قَالَ كُنْ لِقَصْدِنَا قَضَاهُ
If 'Be!' He says, our goals He thus decrees,

وَكُلُّ شَيْءٍ خَالِقِي يَرَاهُ

And everything my Maker plainly sees;

لَا شَيْءَ إِلَّا كَانَ تَحْتَ أَمْرِهِ

Whatever is, is under His Decree,

فِيْ بَرِّهِ أَوْ قَفْرِهِ أَوْ بَحْرِهِ

On land, or in His deserts, or His sea;

وَدَبَّرَ الْأُمُورَ لِلْجَمِيعِ

And all affairs He's managed, as we see,

بِعِلْمِهِ وَصُنْعِهِ الْبَدِيعِ

With knowledge and amazing novelty;

رَفَعْتُ رَاحَتَيَّ لِلْكَرِيمِ

The Noble One, to Him I raised my plea,

مُؤَمِّلاً فِي فَضْلِهِ الْعَظِيمِ

With hope in His great liberality;

أَجَابَنِي فَإِنَّهُ مُجِيبُ

He answered me: He truly does Reply,

وَشَاهِدٌ وَسَامِعٌ قَرِيبُ

And Witnesses, and Hears, and He's Nearby;

فَلَا أَرَى بَعْدَ دُعَاءِ الْبَارِي

I've called my Maker, hence may I not see,

شَدَائِدَ الْأُمورِ بِالْإِعْسَارِ

In my affairs and days, severity!

ظَنِّي جَمِيلٌ فِيكَ يَا عَطُوف
My view of You, O Refuge, is sublime,

حَقِّقْ لِظَنِّي فِيكَ يَا رَءُوف
Confirm for me my view, O Most Benign!

جُنْدِي وَنَاصِرِي هُوَ الرَّحْمٰنُ
My Army, and my Helper, He's Most Kind:

اَلْقَادِرُ الْمُقْتَدِرُ الدَّيَّانُ
The Powerful, Determiner, Divine;

حِصْنِي تَوَكُّلِي عَلَى الرَّقِيبِ
My trust in He Who Watches is my fort:

الْحَافِظِ الْمُحِيطِ وَالْقَرِيبِ
Preserving, All-Embracing, Near Resort;

بِوَجْهِكَ الْعَظِيمِ ذِي الْجَلَالِ
Majestic One, it's to Your Splendid Face,

أَعُوذُ مِنْ مَكَائِدِ الرِّجَالِ
I flee from ruses of the human race,

وَكُلِّ سَاحِرٍ لَهُ أَسْحَارُ
And each magician armed with his black art,

وَكُلِّ غَادِرٍ لَهُ أَشْرَارُ
And every traitor with an evil heart!

يَرُدُّ عَنِّي خَالِقِي أَذَاهُمْ
Away from me their harm My Maker holds:

هُوَ الْعَلِيُّ حَاضِرٌ يَرَاهُمْ

He's High, yet with us, and each thing beholds.

بِاسْمٍ عَظِيمٍ أَعْظَمٍ مَصُونِ

And by the Greatest Name, the one that's hidden,

مُقَدَّسٍ مُعَظَّمٍ مَكْنُونِ

The Holy and Tremendous, the Forbidden,

أَنْزَلْتَهُ فِي مُحْكَمِ الْكِتَابِ

You sent it in the Book, the well established,

عَلَّمْتَهُ لِخُلَّصِ الْأَحْبَابِ

You taught it to Your close ones, Your beloveds,

اللهُ يَا رَحِيمُ يَا رَحْمٰنُ

Allāh, O Gracious Lord, O Most Benign,

يَا عَالِمَ الْغُيُوبِ يَا دَيَّانُ

O Knower of what's hidden, O Divine,

يَا حَيُّ يَا قَيُّومُ يَا مُغِيثُ

O Living, O Sustainer, O Support,

بِرَحْمَتِكَ يَا رَبِّ أَسْتَغِيثُ

It's through Your Mercy that I seek support,

عَجِّلْ بِعَوْنِي يَا مُجِيبَ الدَّاعِي

Be swift, O You Who answers, with Your aid!

هَيِّئْ لَنَا لِقَاءَ خَيْرِ دَاعِي

Prepare us so we meet the best You've made ﷺ,

نَزُورُهُ زِيَارَةً يَرْضَاهَا

And visit him: may he be satisfied,

وَتَفْرَحُ الْأَرْوَاحُ إِذْ نَادَاهَا

And we, through hearing him, be gratified!

اِغْفِرْ لَنَا وَكُلَّ مَنْ تَوَسَّلْ

Forgive us, and whoever seeks to You

بِأَحْمَدٍ نَبِيِّكَ الْمُفَضَّلْ

A means through Prophet Aḥmad, bless'd by You!

مُحَمَّدٌ شَفِيعُنَا الْمَقْبُولُ

Muḥammad's intercession is accepted:

هُوَ النَّبِيُّ الصَّادِقُ الرَّسُولُ

The truthful Prophet, Messenger selected;

صَلَّى عَلَيْهِ رَبُّنَا وَسَلَّمَا

May he be granted peace, our Lord, and bless

وَآلِهِ الْأَطْهَارِ ثُمَّ كَرَّمَا

His Family, the pure, in their noblesse!

وَاجْعَلْ إِلٰهِي دَائِماً رِضَاكَ

And be content, my God, without a break,

لِصَحْبِهِ وَكُلِّ مَنْ وَالَاكَ

With his Companions, and the Friends You take,

وَالتَّابِعِينَ الشِّرْعَةَ الْمَرْضِيَّةَ

And those who to Your pleasing Law adhere,

اَلْمُخْلِصِينَ قَوْلَهُمْ وَالنِّيَّة

With speech and with intention that's sincere!

وَاغْفِرْ إِلٰهِي ذَنْبَ مَنْ دَعَاكَ

Forgive, my God, all those who to You pray

بِهٰذِهِ الدَّعْوَةِ أَوْ نَاجَاكَ

Out loud, or softly, with these lines today!

وَالْجَعْفَرِيُّ صَالِحٌ يَدْعُوكَ

Al-Jaʿfarī, named Ṣāliḥ, calls to You,

عِنْدَ الشَّفِيعِ خَالِقِي يَرْجُوكَ

And, by the Intercessor, hopes in You;

فَكُنْ (لَنَا) يَا رَبِّ بِالْإِحْسَانِ

So deal with (us), O Lord, with excellence

وَاخْتِمْ (لَنَا) بِخَاتِمِ الْإِيْمَانِ

And seal (our lives) with faith, the best of ends!

وَالْآلِ وَالْأَصْحَابِ وَالْأَحْبَابِ

(Our) families, companions and beloveds:

وَفِّقْهُمْ يَا رَبِّ لِلصَّوَابِ

In doing good, let them be well established![5]

5 In the original it said "him" rather than "us" and "his" rather than "our."

Ninety-Nine Names of Allah

﴿هُوَ اللهُ الَّذِي لا إِلَهَ إِلاَّ هُوَ﴾

He is Allāh, none is worthy of being worshiped but Him

الرحمن
ar-Raḥmān
The All-Merciful

الرحيم
ar-Raḥīm
The Most-Merciful

الملك
al-Malik
The Absolute Ruler

القدوس
al-Quddūs
The Absolutely Pure

السلام
as-Salām
The Source of Peace

المؤمن
al-Mu'min
The Source of Security

المهيمن
al-Muhaymin
The Protector

العزيز
al-ʿAzīz
The Mighty

الجبار
al-Jabbār
The Compeller

المتكبر
al-Mutakabbir
The Greatest

الخالق
al-Khāliq
The Creator

البارئ
al-Bāri'
The Maker

المصور
al-Muṣawwir
The Fashioner

الغفار
al-Ghaffār
The Ever Forgiving

القهار
al-Qahhār
The Subduer

الوهاب
al-Wahhāb
The Giver

الرزاق
al-Razzāq
The Provider

الفتاح
al-Fattāḥ
The Opener

العليم
al-ʿAlīm
The All-Knowing

القابض
al-Qābiḍ
The Constrictor

الباسط
al-Bāsiṭ
The Reliever

الخافض
al-Khāfiḍ
The Abaser

الرافع

ar-Rāfiʿ

The Exalter

المعز

al-Muʿizz

The Honourer

المذل

al-Mudhill

The Humbler

السميع

as-Samīʿ

The All-Hearing

البصير

al-Baṣīr

The All-Seeing

الحكم

al-Ḥakam

The Judge

العدل

al-ʿAdl

The Just

اللطيف

al-Laṭīf

The Kind

الخبير

al-Khabīr

The All-Aware

الحليم

al-Ḥalīm

The Clement

العظيم

al-ʿAẓīm

The Immense

الغفور

al-Ghafūr

The All-Forgiving

الشكور

ash-Shakūr

The Rewarder

العلي

al-ʿAlī

The Most High

الكبير

al-Kabīr

The Most Great

الحفيظ

al-Ḥafīẓ

The Preserver

المقيت

al-Muqīt

The Sustainer

الحسيب

al-Ḥasīb

The Reckoner

الجليل

al-Jalīl

The Majestic

الكريم

al-Karīm

The Generous

الرقيب

ar-Raqīb

The Watcher

المجيب

al-Mujīb

The Answerer

الواسع

al-Wāsiʿ

The Vast

الحكيم

al-Ḥakīm

The Wise

الودود

al-Wadūd

The Loving

المجيد

al-Majīd

The Glorious

الباعث

al-Bāʿith

The Resurrector

الشهيد

ash-Shahīd

The Witness

الحق
al-Ḥaqq
The Truth

الوكيل
al-Wakīl
The Trustee

القوي
al-Qawī
The Powerful

المتين
al-Matīn
The Firm

الولي
al-Walī
The Loving Supporter

الحميد
al-Ḥamīd
The Praiseworthy

المحصي
al-Muḥṣī
The Counter

المبدئ
al-Mubdiʾ
The Originator

المعيد
al-Muʿīd
The Restorer

المحيي
al-Muḥyī
The Giver of Life

المميت
al-Mumīt
The Taker of Life

الحي
al-Ḥayy
The Ever Living

القيوم
al-Qayyūm
The Self-Sustaining

الواجد
al-Wājid
The Finder

الماجد

al-Mājid

The Noble

الواحد

al-Wāḥid

The One

الصمد

aṣ-Ṣamad

The Eternal Refuge

القادر

al-Qādir

The All-Capable

المقتدر

al-Muqtadir

The Prevailing

المقدم

al-Muqaddim

The Expediter

المؤخر

al-Mu'akh-khir

The Delayer

الأول

al-Awwal

The First

الآخر

al-Ākhir

The Last

الظاهر

aẓ-Ẓāhir

The Manifest One

الباطن

al-Bāṭin

The Hidden One

الوالي

al-Wālī

The Guardian

المتعالي

al-Mutaʿālī

The Supreme

البر

al-Barr

The Good

التواب

at-Tawwāb

The Acceptor of Repentance

المنتقم

al-Muntaqim

The Avenger

العفو

al-ʿAfū

The Pardoner

الرؤوف

ar-Raʾūf

The Compassionate

مالك الملك

Māliku l-Mulk

The Owner of all

ذو الجلال والإكرام

Dhu l-jalāli wa-l-ikrām

Lord of Majesty and Honour

المقسط

al-Muqsiṭ

The Equitable

الجامع

al-Jāmiʿ

The Gatherer

الغني

al-Ghanī

The Rich

المغني

al-Mughnī

The Enricher

المانع

al-Māniʿ

The Withholder

الضار

aḍ-Ḍārr

The Afflicter

النافع

an-Nāfiʿ

The Benefactor

النور

an-Nūr

The Light

الهادي *al-Hādī* The Guide	البديع *al-Badīʿ* The Incomparable
الباقي *al-Bāqī* The Everlasting	الوارث *al-Wārith* The Inheritor of All
الرشيد *ar-Rashīd* The Guide to the Right Path	الصبور *aṣ-Ṣabūr* The Most Patient

اللهُمَّ إنِّيْ أَسأَلُكَ نُوراً مِنْ أَنْوارِهَا وأَنْ تُنَوِّرْ بِهَا بَصَرِي
وَتَهْدِي بِهَا قَلْبِي وَتُوَفِّقَنِي بِهَا إِلَى الْخَيْرِ، وَتَعْزِمْ بِهَا عَلَيَّ
أَرْشَدَ أَمْرِي

O Allāh I ask You for a light from the light of these Names, and that You illuminate my sight and guide my heart through them. O Allāh I ask You to help me do that which is good and to direct me to stay firm upon the most righteous way in all my affairs

الحُصُونُ القُرْآنِيَّة

The Qur'ānic Defences

This is a selection of Qur'ānic verses that was used by the Prophet ﷺ to cure a man and protect him from some type of psychological or spiritual harm that had befallen him (see *Sunan Ibn Mājah*, Book of Medicine; *Mustadrak al-Ḥākim*, Book of Protective Incantations (*ruqā*) and Amulets). Shaykh Ṣāliḥ chose them as a daily litany of protection, which he called The Qur'ānic Defences (*al-ḥuṣūn al-Qur'āniyya*).

﴿بِسْمِ ٱللَّهِ ٱلرَّحْمَٰنِ ٱلرَّحِيمِ ۝١ ٱلْحَمْدُ لِلَّهِ رَبِّ ٱلْعَٰلَمِينَ ۝٢
ٱلرَّحْمَٰنِ ٱلرَّحِيمِ ۝٣ مَٰلِكِ يَوْمِ ٱلدِّينِ ۝٤ إِيَّاكَ نَعْبُدُ وَإِيَّاكَ
نَسْتَعِينُ ۝٥ ٱهْدِنَا ٱلصِّرَٰطَ ٱلْمُسْتَقِيمَ ۝٦ صِرَٰطَ ٱلَّذِينَ
أَنْعَمْتَ عَلَيْهِمْ غَيْرِ ٱلْمَغْضُوبِ عَلَيْهِمْ وَلَا ٱلضَّآلِّينَ﴾[6]

﴿الٓمٓ ۝١ ذَٰلِكَ ٱلْكِتَٰبُ لَا رَيْبَ ۛ فِيهِ ۛ هُدًى لِّلْمُتَّقِينَ ۝٢
ٱلَّذِينَ يُؤْمِنُونَ بِٱلْغَيْبِ وَيُقِيمُونَ ٱلصَّلَوٰةَ وَمِمَّا رَزَقْنَٰهُمْ
يُنفِقُونَ ۝٣ وَٱلَّذِينَ يُؤْمِنُونَ بِمَآ أُنزِلَ إِلَيْكَ وَمَآ أُنزِلَ مِن

6 Sūrat al-Fātiḥah, 1:1-7

قَبْلِكَ وَبِٱلْـَٔاخِرَةِ هُمْ يُوقِنُونَ ﴿٤﴾ أُو۟لَـٰٓئِكَ عَلَىٰ هُدًى مِّن
رَّبِّهِمْ ۖ وَأُو۟لَـٰٓئِكَ هُمُ ٱلْمُفْلِحُونَ﴾[7]

﴿وَإِلَـٰهُكُمْ إِلَـٰهٌ وَٰحِدٌ ۖ لَّآ إِلَـٰهَ إِلَّا هُوَ ٱلرَّحْمَـٰنُ ٱلرَّحِيمُ ﴿١٦٣﴾
إِنَّ فِى خَلْقِ ٱلسَّمَـٰوَٰتِ وَٱلْأَرْضِ وَٱخْتِلَـٰفِ ٱلَّيْلِ وَٱلنَّهَارِ
وَٱلْفُلْكِ ٱلَّتِى تَجْرِى فِى ٱلْبَحْرِ بِمَا يَنفَعُ ٱلنَّاسَ وَمَآ أَنزَلَ
ٱللَّهُ مِنَ ٱلسَّمَآءِ مِن مَّآءٍ فَأَحْيَا بِهِ ٱلْأَرْضَ بَعْدَ مَوْتِهَا وَبَثَّ
فِيهَا مِن كُلِّ دَآبَّةٍ وَتَصْرِيفِ ٱلرِّيَـٰحِ وَٱلسَّحَابِ ٱلْمُسَخَّرِ
بَيْنَ ٱلسَّمَآءِ وَٱلْأَرْضِ لَـَٔايَـٰتٍ لِّقَوْمٍ يَعْقِلُونَ﴾[8]

﴿ٱللَّهُ لَآ إِلَـٰهَ إِلَّا هُوَ ٱلْحَىُّ ٱلْقَيُّومُ ۚ لَا تَأْخُذُهُۥ سِنَةٌ وَلَا نَوْمٌ ۚ
لَّهُۥ مَا فِى ٱلسَّمَـٰوَٰتِ وَمَا فِى ٱلْأَرْضِ ۗ مَن ذَا ٱلَّذِى يَشْفَعُ عِندَهُۥٓ
إِلَّا بِإِذْنِهِۦ ۚ يَعْلَمُ مَا بَيْنَ أَيْدِيهِمْ وَمَا خَلْفَهُمْ ۖ وَلَا يُحِيطُونَ
بِشَىْءٍ مِّنْ عِلْمِهِۦٓ إِلَّا بِمَا شَآءَ ۚ وَسِعَ كُرْسِيُّهُ ٱلسَّمَـٰوَٰتِ
وَٱلْأَرْضَ ۖ وَلَا يَـُٔودُهُۥ حِفْظُهُمَا ۚ وَهُوَ ٱلْعَلِىُّ ٱلْعَظِيمُ﴾[9]

﴿ءَامَنَ ٱلرَّسُولُ بِمَآ أُنزِلَ إِلَيْهِ مِن رَّبِّهِۦ وَٱلْمُؤْمِنُونَ ۚ كُلٌّ
ءَامَنَ بِٱللَّهِ وَمَلَـٰٓئِكَتِهِۦ وَكُتُبِهِۦ وَرُسُلِهِۦ لَا نُفَرِّقُ بَيْنَ
أَحَدٍ مِّن رُّسُلِهِۦ ۚ وَقَالُوا۟ سَمِعْنَا وَأَطَعْنَا ۖ غُفْرَانَكَ رَبَّنَا

7 Sūrat al-Baqarah, 2:1-5
8 Sūrat al-Baqarah, 2:163-164
9 Sūrat al-Baqarah, 2:255

وَإِلَيْكَ ٱلْمَصِيرُ ﴿٢٨٥﴾ لَا يُكَلِّفُ ٱللَّهُ نَفْسًا إِلَّا وُسْعَهَا ۚ لَهَا
مَا كَسَبَتْ وَعَلَيْهَا مَا ٱكْتَسَبَتْ ۗ رَبَّنَا لَا تُؤَاخِذْنَآ إِن
نَّسِينَآ أَوْ أَخْطَأْنَا ۚ رَبَّنَا وَلَا تَحْمِلْ عَلَيْنَآ إِصْرًا كَمَا حَمَلْتَهُۥ
عَلَى ٱلَّذِينَ مِن قَبْلِنَا ۚ رَبَّنَا وَلَا تُحَمِّلْنَا مَا لَا طَاقَةَ لَنَا بِهِۦ ۖ
وَٱعْفُ عَنَّا وَٱغْفِرْ لَنَا وَٱرْحَمْنَآ ۚ أَنتَ مَوْلَىٰنَا فَٱنصُرْنَا عَلَى
ٱلْقَوْمِ ٱلْكَٰفِرِينَ﴾[10]

﴿شَهِدَ ٱللَّهُ أَنَّهُۥ لَآ إِلَٰهَ إِلَّا هُوَ وَٱلْمَلَٰٓئِكَةُ وَأُولُوا ٱلْعِلْمِ
قَآئِمًۢا بِٱلْقِسْطِ ۚ لَآ إِلَٰهَ إِلَّا هُوَ ٱلْعَزِيزُ ٱلْحَكِيمُ﴾[11]

﴿إِنَّ رَبَّكُمُ ٱللَّهُ ٱلَّذِى خَلَقَ ٱلسَّمَٰوَٰتِ وَٱلْأَرْضَ فِى سِتَّةِ
أَيَّامٍ ثُمَّ ٱسْتَوَىٰ عَلَى ٱلْعَرْشِ يُغْشِى ٱلَّيْلَ ٱلنَّهَارَ يَطْلُبُهُۥ
حَثِيثًا وَٱلشَّمْسَ وَٱلْقَمَرَ وَٱلنُّجُومَ مُسَخَّرَٰتٍۭ بِأَمْرِهِۦٓ ۗ أَلَا لَهُ
ٱلْخَلْقُ وَٱلْأَمْرُ ۗ تَبَارَكَ ٱللَّهُ رَبُّ ٱلْعَٰلَمِينَ﴾[12]

﴿أَفَحَسِبْتُمْ أَنَّمَا خَلَقْنَٰكُمْ عَبَثًا وَأَنَّكُمْ إِلَيْنَا لَا
تُرْجَعُونَ ﴿١١٥﴾ فَتَعَٰلَى ٱللَّهُ ٱلْمَلِكُ ٱلْحَقُّ ۖ لَآ إِلَٰهَ إِلَّا هُوَ رَبُّ
ٱلْعَرْشِ ٱلْكَرِيمِ ﴿١١٦﴾ وَمَن يَدْعُ مَعَ ٱللَّهِ إِلَٰهًا ءَاخَرَ لَا بُرْهَٰنَ

10 Sūrat al-Baqarah, 2:285-286
11 Sūrat Āli ʿImrān, 3:18
12 Sūrat al-Aʿrāf, 7:54

لَهُۥ بِهِۦ فَإِنَّمَا حِسَابُهُۥ عِندَ رَبِّهِۦٓ ۚ إِنَّهُۥ لَا يُفْلِحُ ٱلْكَٰفِرُونَ
۝١١٧ وَقُل رَّبِّ ٱغْفِرْ وَٱرْحَمْ وَأَنتَ خَيْرُ ٱلرَّٰحِمِينَ﴾[13]

﴿وَٱلصَّٰٓفَّٰتِ صَفًّا ۝١ فَٱلزَّٰجِرَٰتِ زَجْرًا ۝٢ فَٱلتَّٰلِيَٰتِ ذِكْرًا
۝٣ إِنَّ إِلَٰهَكُمْ لَوَٰحِدٌ ۝٤ رَّبُّ ٱلسَّمَٰوَٰتِ وَٱلْأَرْضِ وَمَا بَيْنَهُمَا
وَرَبُّ ٱلْمَشَٰرِقِ ۝٥ إِنَّا زَيَّنَّا ٱلسَّمَآءَ ٱلدُّنْيَا بِزِينَةٍ ٱلْكَوَاكِبِ ۝٦
وَحِفْظًا مِّن كُلِّ شَيْطَٰنٍ مَّارِدٍ ۝٧ لَّا يَسَّمَّعُونَ إِلَى ٱلْمَلَإِ ٱلْأَعْلَىٰ
وَيُقْذَفُونَ مِن كُلِّ جَانِبٍ ۝٨ دُحُورًا ۖ وَلَهُمْ عَذَابٌ وَاصِبٌ ۝٩
إِلَّا مَنْ خَطِفَ ٱلْخَطْفَةَ فَأَتْبَعَهُۥ شِهَابٌ ثَاقِبٌ﴾[14]

﴿لَوْ أَنزَلْنَا هَٰذَا ٱلْقُرْءَانَ عَلَىٰ جَبَلٍ لَّرَأَيْتَهُۥ خَٰشِعًا مُّتَصَدِّعًا
مِّنْ خَشْيَةِ ٱللَّهِ ۚ وَتِلْكَ ٱلْأَمْثَٰلُ نَضْرِبُهَا لِلنَّاسِ لَعَلَّهُمْ
يَتَفَكَّرُونَ ۝٢٢ هُوَ ٱللَّهُ ٱلَّذِى لَآ إِلَٰهَ إِلَّا هُوَ ۖ عَٰلِمُ ٱلْغَيْبِ
وَٱلشَّهَٰدَةِ ۖ هُوَ ٱلرَّحْمَٰنُ ٱلرَّحِيمُ ۝٢٣ هُوَ ٱللَّهُ ٱلَّذِى لَآ إِلَٰهَ إِلَّا
هُوَ ٱلْمَلِكُ ٱلْقُدُّوسُ ٱلسَّلَٰمُ ٱلْمُؤْمِنُ ٱلْمُهَيْمِنُ ٱلْعَزِيزُ ٱلْجَبَّارُ
ٱلْمُتَكَبِّرُ ۚ سُبْحَٰنَ ٱللَّهِ عَمَّا يُشْرِكُونَ ۝٢٤ هُوَ ٱللَّهُ ٱلْخَٰلِقُ
ٱلْبَارِئُ ٱلْمُصَوِّرُ ۖ لَهُ ٱلْأَسْمَآءُ ٱلْحُسْنَىٰ ۚ يُسَبِّحُ لَهُۥ مَا فِى
ٱلسَّمَٰوَٰتِ وَٱلْأَرْضِ ۖ وَهُوَ ٱلْعَزِيزُ ٱلْحَكِيمُ﴾[15]

13 Sūrat al-Mu'minūn, 23:115-118
14 Sūrat al-Ṣāffāt, 37:1-10
15 Sūrat al-Ḥashr, 59:21-24

﴿وَأَنَّهُۥ تَعَـٰلَىٰ جَدُّ رَبِّنَا مَا ٱتَّخَذَ صَـٰحِبَةً وَلَا وَلَدًا﴾[16]

﴿قُلْ هُوَ ٱللَّهُ أَحَدٌ ۝١ ٱللَّهُ ٱلصَّمَدُ ۝٢ لَمْ يَلِدْ وَلَمْ يُولَدْ ۝٣
وَلَمْ يَكُن لَّهُۥ كُفُوًا أَحَدٌۢ﴾[17]

﴿قُلْ أَعُوذُ بِرَبِّ ٱلْفَلَقِ ۝١ مِن شَرِّ مَا خَلَقَ ۝٢ وَمِن شَرِّ
غَاسِقٍ إِذَا وَقَبَ ۝٣ وَمِن شَرِّ ٱلنَّفَّـٰثَـٰتِ فِى ٱلْعُقَدِ ۝٤ وَمِن
شَرِّ حَاسِدٍ إِذَا حَسَدَ﴾[18]

﴿قُلْ أَعُوذُ بِرَبِّ ٱلنَّاسِ ۝١ مَلِكِ ٱلنَّاسِ ۝٢ إِلَـٰهِ ٱلنَّاسِ ۝٣
مِن شَرِّ ٱلْوَسْوَاسِ ٱلْخَنَّاسِ ۝٤ ٱلَّذِى يُوَسْوِسُ فِى صُدُورِ
ٱلنَّاسِ ۝٥ مِنَ ٱلْجِنَّةِ وَٱلنَّاسِ﴾[19]

16 Sūrat al-Jinn, 72:3
17 Sūrat al-Ikhlāṣ, 112:1-4
18 Sūrat al-Falaq, 113:1-5
19 Sūrat al-Nās, 114:1-6

الْمَحَامِدُ الْجَعْفَرِيَّة

Supplications of Praise

بِسْمِ اللهِ الرَّحْمٰنِ الرَّحِيمِ
وَصَلَّى اللهُ عَلَى سَيِّدِنَا مُحَمَّدٍ وَعَلَى آلِهِ
فِي كُلِّ لَمْحَةٍ وَنَفَسٍ عَدَدَ مَا وَسِعَهُ عِلْمُ اللهِ

In the name of Allāh, the All-Merciful the Most-Merciful
And may Allāh exalt our master Muhammad and his Folk,
with every glance and breath, as many as are contained in the knowledge of Allāh.

اَللَّهُمَّ لَكَ الْحَمْدُ حَمْدًا أَسْتَزِيدُ بِهِ مِنْ نِعَمِكَ فِي حَيَاتِي

O Allāh, for You alone is praise; a declaration of praise by which I seek an increase of Your blessings in my life,

وَ أَنْعَمُ بِهِ بَعْدَ مَمَاتِي

and by which I am blessed after my death,

حَمْدًا أَرَى بِهِ خُرُوْجَ رُوحِي مُيَسَّرًا

a praise by which I see my spirit separated
(from my body) with ease,

وَ أَرَى بِهِ قَبْرِي مُنَوَّرًا

and by which I see my grave illuminated.

اَللَّهُمَّ لَكَ الْحَمْدُ حَمْدًا لَا يَنْقَطِعُ ثَوَابُهُ إِذَا دُفِنْتُ تَحْتَ التُّرَابِ

O Allāh, for You alone is praise; a declaration of praise whose
reward will not be cut off when I am buried under dust,

وَ أَكُوْنُ بِهِ آمِنًا مِنْ كُلِّ شَرٍّ وَعَذَابِ

and by which I am safe from every evil and torment.

اَللَّهُمَّ لَكَ الْحَمْدُ حَمْدًا تَمُنُّ بِهِ عَلَيَّ بِأُنْسِكَ فِي خَلْوَتِي

O Allāh, for You alone is praise; a declaration of praise by which
You bless me with Your intimacy in my seclusion,

وَعِنْدَ حُلُولِي بِقَبْرِي وَوِحْدَتِي

and when I am enclosed in my grave, alone.

اَللَّهُمَّ لَكَ الْحَمْدُ حَمْدًا يَكُونُ لِي حِصْنًا عَنْ مَعَاصِيكَ

O Allāh, for You alone is praise; a declaration of praise which will
be, for me, a protection against disobeying You,

وَثَبَاتًا لِي عِنْدَ قُرْبِكَ وَتَجَلِّيكَ

and a support for me in the experience of Your Nearness and
Your Self-disclosure.

اَللَّهُمَّ لَكَ الْحَمْدُ حَمْدًا يَكُونُ لِي أَمَانًا مِنْ غَضَبِكَ
وَسَخَطِكَ

O Allāh, for You alone is praise; a declaration of praise which grants me safety from Your anger and Your displeasure,

وَأَنالُ بِهِ حَلَاوَةَ تِلَاوَةِ كِتَابِكَ وَذِكْرِكَ

and because of which I attain the sweetness of reciting Your Book, and of Your remembrance.

اَللَّهُمَّ لَكَ الْحَمْدُ حَمْدًا أَكُوْنُ آمِنًا بِهِ مِنْ زَوَالِ النِّعْمَةِ

O Allāh, for You alone is praise; a declaration of praise by which I am secure from the removal of blessings,

وَفُجَاءَةِ النِّقْمَةِ

and from Your sudden wrath,

وَتَحَوُّلِ عَافِيَتِكَ

and from change in Your bestowal of well-being,

وَأَنالُ بِهِ أَسْرَارًا مِنْ عُلُومِ كِتَابِكَ وَحِكْمَتِكَ

and by which I obtain the secrets of the sciences of Your Book and Your Wisdom.

اَللَّهُمَّ لَكَ الْحَمْدُ حَمْدًا أَنَالُ بِهِ الْإِقْبَالَ عَلَيْكَ

O Allāh, for You alone is praise; a declaration of praise by which I am drawn towards You with my whole self,

وَ تَفْوِيضَ أُمُورِي إِلَيْكَ

and by which I surrender my affairs to You.

اَللَّهُمَّ لَكَ الْحَمْدُ حَمْدًا أَنالُ بِهِ عَفْوَكَ وَمَغْفِرَتَكَ

O Allāh, for You alone is praise; a declaration of praise by which I obtain Your pardon and Your forgiveness,

لِي وَلِوَالِدَيَّ

for myself and for my parents,

وَ لِلْمُؤْمِنِينَ وَالْمُؤْمِنَاتِ

and for the believing men and the believing women,

وَالْمُسْلِمِينَ وَالْمُسْلِمَاتِ

and the Muslim men and the Muslim women,

الْأَحْيَاءِ مِنْهُمْ وَالْأَمْوَاتِ

those of them who are living, and those of them who have died.

صَلَاةُ الْفَرَجِ الْعَجِيبْ وَالْفَتْحِ الْقَرِيب

The Prayer of Wondrous Relief & Quick Opening

Shaykh ʿAbd al-Ghanī al-Jaʿfarī wrote,

> As for the Prayer of Wondrous Relief and Quick Opening – which is by the Knower of Allāh most high Shaykh Ṣāliḥ al-Jaʿfarī – its virtue can be known from its name. There is nothing quicker than it for the removal of worries, relief from distress, and expanse in sustenance. As for its share in the world of spiritual elevation and ascent, its secret in bringing about spiritual opening (illumination) is quick, and in arrival at the Messenger of Allāh ﷺ is sure.

اللّٰهُمَّ صَلِّ عَلَى مَنْ أَعْلَيْتَ لَهُ الرُّتَبْ ۞ وَكَشَفْتَ لَهُ
الْحُجُبْ ۞ فَرَقَى إِلَى مَا لَمْ يَرْقَ إِلَيْهِ الْخَلِيلْ ۞ وَوَصَلَ
إِلَى مَا لَمْ يَصِلْ إِلَيْهِ جِبْرِيلْ ۞ وَنَظَرَ مَا لَمْ يَنْظُرْهُ الْكَلِيمْ
۞ وَوَصَفْتَهُ بِأَنَّهُ بِالْمُؤْمِنِينَ رَءُوفٌ رَحِيمْ ۞ وَصَلَّيْتَ
عَلَيهِ أَنْتَ وَمَلَائِكَتُكَ تَحَبُّباً وَتَكرِيمَا ۞ وَقُلْتَ ﴿يَا
أَيُّهَا الَّذِينَ آمَنُوا صَلُّوا عَلَيْهِ وَسَلِّمُوا تَسْلِيمًا﴾ ۞ عَبْدُكَ
وَنَبِيُّكَ وَرَسُولُكَ الْبَشِيرُ النَّذِيرْ ۞ سَيِّدُنَا وَمَوْلَانَا مُحَمَّدُ

بْنُ عَبْدِ اللهِ السِّرَاجُ الْمُنِيرْ ۞ فَصَلِّ اللّٰهُمَّ عَلَيْهِ بِعَدَدِ
صَلَاةِ الْمُصَلِّينَ عَلَيْهِ مِنَ الْخَلْقِ أَجْمَعِينْ ۞ وَعَلَى آلِهِ وَسَلِّمْ
فِي كُلِّ لَمْحَةٍ وَنَفَسٍ بِعَدَدِ كُلِّ مَعْلُومٍ لَكَ آمِينْ ۞ وَارْضَ
اللّٰهُمَّ عَنْ أَهْلِ بَيْتِهِ الطَّاهِرِينَ وَعَنْ أَصْحَابِهِ الطَّيِّبِينْ ۞
وَارْحَمْ أُمَّتَهُ وَاحْفَظْ شَرِيعَتَهُ وَبَارِكْ عَلَيْهِ وَعَلَيْهِمْ إِلَى يَوْمِ
الدِّينْ ۞ اللّٰهُمَّ بِعَظِيمِ فَضْلِكَ وَبِجَاهِهِ عِنْدَكْ ۞ هَبْ لَنَا
مِن لَدُنْكَ رَحْمَةً إِنَّكَ أَنْتَ الْوَهَّابْ ۞ وَافْتَحْ لَنَا مِنَ الْخَيْرِ
كُلَّ بَابْ ۞ يَا مَنْ قَالَ وَقَوْلُهُ الْحَقُّ فِي مُحْكَمِ الْكِتَابْ ۞
﴿إِنَّ اللهَ يَرْزُقُ مَنْ يَشَاءُ بِغَيْرِ حِسَابْ﴾

Allāhumma sallī ʿalā man aʿlayta lahu r-rutab, wa kashafta lahu l-ḥujub, fa-raqā ilā mā-lam yarqa ilayhi l-Khalīl, wa waṣala ilā mā-lam yaṣil ilayhi Jibrīl, wa naẓara mā-lam yanẓurhu l-kalīm, wa waṣaftahū bi-annahū bi-l-muʾminīna raʾūfun raḥīm, wa ṣallayta ʿalayhi anta wa malāʾikatuka taḥabbuban wa takrīmā, wa qulta ﴿yā ayyuha l-ladhīna āmanū ṣallū ʿalayhi wa sallimū taslīma﴾, ʿabduka wa nabiyyuka wa rasūluka l-bashīru n-nadhīr, sayyidunā wa mawlāna Muḥammad-u b-nu ʿAbdillāh-i s-sirāju l-munīr, fa-ṣalli l-Lāhumma ʿalayhi bi-ʿadada ṣalāti l-muṣallīna ʿalayhi mina l-khalqi ajmaʿīn, warḍa l-Lāhumma ʿan ahli baytihi ṭ-ṭāhirīn wa ʿan aṣḥābihī ṭ-ṭayyibīn, warḥam ummatahū waḥfaẓ sharīʿatahū wa bārik ʿalayhi wa ʿalayhim ilā yawmi d-dīn. Allāhumma bi-ʿaẓīmi faḍlika wa bi-jāhihī ʿindak, hab lanā min ladunka raḥmatan innaka anta l-Wahhāb, waftaḥ lanā mina l-khayri kulla bāb, yā man qāla wa qawluhu l-ḥaqqu fī muḥkami l-Kitāb, ﴿inna l-Lāha yarzuqu man yashāʾu bi-ghayri ḥisāb﴾

O Allāh exalt him whose ranks you raised ۞ and for whom you lifted the veils ۞ so he ascended to where Abraham did not ascend ۞ and reached where Gabriel did not reach ۞ and saw what Moses did not see ۞ and whom you described as merciful and compassionate to the believers ۞ and You and Your angels exalted him out of love and honouring ۞ and You said: ﴿*O You who believe (ask Allāh to) exalt him and send him greetings of peace in abundance*﴾ ۞ Your perfect servant, Your Prophet and Your Messenger, the bearer of glad tidings and warnings ۞ our master Muḥammad son of ʿAbdullāh, the luminous lamp ۞ So exalt him O Allāh as many times as the number of times You are asked to exalt him by all Your creation ۞ and exalt his folk and send them all greetings of peace with every breath and every glance ۞ as many times as everything that is known to You! Amen! ۞ And be pleased O Allāh with the pure People of his Household and his good Companions ۞ and show mercy to his community and preserve his Sharīʿah ۞ and bless him and bless them until the Day of Submission ۞ O Allāh we ask You by Your immense grace and by his rank with You ۞ to bestow upon us mercy from Yourself, for You, You are the Bestower ۞ and to open for us every door of goodness ۞ O You who said in the clear Book, and Your speech is the truth: ﴿*Allāh provides for whom He wishes without limit*﴾

NOTES

NOTES

Lightning Source UK Ltd.
Milton Keynes UK
UKOW03f2314010217
293340UK00001B/86/P